A TRIPTYCH OF POISONERS

None knew the components of that subtle draught which the Borgias were apt to slip into the wine of those they considered to be their enemies. All were sure that it could provide death in some form or another. Some men, after partaking of it, appeared to go into a drunken sleep from which they did not wake; others went merrily away to be seized by violent agony during the night and die before the dawn broke; some contracted a lingering illness which did not affect them until weeks later. They went into declines; their hair fell out; their nails dropped off, and their teeth broke as if they had become as brittle as glass.

Also by Jean Plaidy in *Star*

MARY QUEEN OF SCOTS
THE RISE OF THE SPANISH INQUISITION
THE GROWTH OF THE SPANISH INQUISITION
THE END OF THE SPANISH INQUISITION
THE SPANISH INQUISITION OMNIBUS

A TRIPTYCH OF POISONERS

Jean Plaidy

A STAR BOOK
published by
the Paperback Division of
W. H. ALLEN & Co. Ltd

A Star Book
Published in 1979
by the Paperback Division of
W. H. Allen & Co. Ltd
A Howard and Wyndham Company
44 Hill Street, London W1X 8LB

First published in Great Britain by Robert Hale, 1958

Copyright © Jean Plaidy, 1958

Printed in Great Britain by
Hazell Watson & Viney Ltd, Aylesbury, Bucks

ISBN 0 352 30347 6

CONTENTS

THE MOTIVE

CRIMINALS IN the past have been treated harshly—far too harshly, most will agree. It is not very long ago when a man could be hanged for stealing a sheep, and there are heart-rending stories of little children who have suffered the extreme penalty for no other reason than that they stole food when they were hungry. Hangings were barbarously conducted in public; and it was only reasonable that, with the advance of civilization, this practice should fill normal people with disgust, and be discontinued.

The guilt of our ancestors rests heavily upon our shoulders, and it is fashionable to say when crime is discussed: "The guilt of the criminal is the guilt of us all."

There was some truth in this in the days of Victoria. Those who rode in their carriages and saw the starving people in the gutters, those who were aware of the terrible conditions prevailing in the rookeries of St. Giles's and such districts, those who thoughtlessly delighted in their delicately embroidered gowns, accepting the fact that those who had made them were stitching at once with a double thread a shroud as well as a gown, and those who were aware of the conditions in the mines and mills of their country, if they did nothing to improve these conditions, *were* the guilty ones.

I should accept my guilt if I had lived in those days—unless, of course, I had been a Charles Dickens, a George Eliot, a Thomas Hood or an Elizabeth Fry.

But no one can deny that conditions in England have now changed, and it occurred to me that it might be interesting to examine that cliché: "The guilt belongs to us all."

There are many vicious people in the world, and it may well be that their tragic and useless lives have been the direct result of environment and that the most respectable of us should say: "There, but for the grace of God, go I." It may well be that someone in the world might have saved some desperate criminal from being what he is; but that is the guilt of that particular person, not the guilt of us all.

Murder is the greatest of all crimes because it destroys what is more precious than that which is to be found in a bank or a jeweller's shop. The life of each person is quite different from that of any other; therefore the murderer has destroyed something which is unique; and he has committed this criminal act because this unique thing—precious to at least one other—stood between him and his pleasure, comfort or desire.

To assure myself that this guilt theory is out-dated, I decided to look more closely at this crime. In studying the *murderer*, I would not select the person who kills in sudden rage, but the one who plans calmly, malignantly, to destroy the life of another. I wondered whether such people are murderers by nature, and whether the seeds of this most terrible of all crimes are within them waiting to be nourished by lust, envy, greed or any other of the seven deadly sins. If this is so, these people are not entirely sane—I use the word in the original sense—for their mental vision would be at fault, and it is, unfortunately, not so easy to cure a mental defect as it is a physical one.

If people are born with a tendency to murder, all those who have committed this crime should, it seems, have at least one characteristic in common; and, in an endeavour to discover if this is so, I have selected three murderers, from different countries, living in three entirely different environments. I have studied their motives, their actions and their characters in search of this similarity which might lead me to discover what made them become murderers.

Each of the people under review committed more than one murder, and my motive is to discover what made them act as they did, and to ask myself whether they, in other circumstances, would have lived as normal people. If they would have done so, then one must say: "In another environment, in different circumstances, they would not have murdered." Then the guilt must be shared by others who made the circumstances and the environment. If on the other hand one can say: "These people were born to be murderers. In any other environment they would have done the same when some obstacle to their lust, greed, desire, etc., loomed in their path", then the guilt is wholly theirs.

When I reach my summing up, I hope to have discovered whether the guilt for the crimes these people committed was in themselves or in their world. This, I think and hope, may be arrived at by a close inspection, not so much of their deeds as of their characters.

The study of murderers has always been of interest to a great many people; therefore I am setting out my analyses in these three short biographical sketches of notorious murderers, and I hope that my readers will find this study as absorbing as I have.

CESARE BORGIA

STUDENTS OF history often disagree about facts, dates and the spelling of names; and it is impossible to say for sure what was the exact birthdate of a person as notorious even as Cesare Borgia. He may have been born in the years 1476, 1475 or 1474. I do not think that the date is of any great significance in this case. It is not important to state the exact age when Cesare became his sister's lover, made the wife of one of his brothers his mistress, or murdered another brother; it is only relevant to say that he committed these acts, for it was such that made of him one of the most cruel, lascivious and unnatural men who ever lived.

It is necessary, however, before judging this man, to compare the world in which he was living with the present day, to glance at his upbringing, and to see whether the reason for his hideous record sprang from heredity or environment.

For instance, if Cesare had been born in this century and grew up under the solicitous care of kindly parents who taught him how to lead a good life, and whose great desire was to set him up in a prosperous and not too adventurous career, would he be similar to many young men who usefully inhabit our twentieth century?

I think not, for Cesare was cursed with the myopia of the criminal. He saw himself as through a telescope, magnified out of all proportion; when he looked at other people it is as though he turned the telescope round to do so. He saw the people about him as midgets—less—no more than gnats or moths to be crushed to death or exterminated with insecticide.

Yet it must be remembered that Cesare was born into a world of intrigue, ambition and of a cruelty which was so careless that it was deemed natural. Because he was his father's son, he was born to power, and because of his character he became the dominant member in a corrupt and unscrupulous family.

*   *   *

First look at his parents. He was the illegitimate son of Roderigo Borgia—at the time of Cesare's birth a Cardinal and later to become Pope Alexander VI—and Vannozza Cattanei, a woman of Rome.

The Borgias came from Spain, and they were outstanding for their beauty, their virility, their ambition and their striking mental ability. They claimed descent from the Kings of Aragon and their bearing was royal.

Alfonso Borgia first came to Naples in the service of Alfonso of Aragon, and there was created a Cardinal. Spain at this time was determined to dominate Europe, and one of its great ambitions was to see a Spanish Pope in the Vatican.

Alfonso Borgia was elected Pope in 1455 and, as Calixtus III, immediately began to look about him to see what plums of office he could place in the hands of his kinsmen—of whom he had many. Family feeling ran high among the Borgias; they admired each other more than they admired any other people in the world. This family devotion took a sinister turn in a later generation of Borgias, when father, sons and daughter were so enamoured of each other that they were accused of incest: Cesare was suspected of being the father of one of Lucrezia's children, and Lucrezia was called her father's 'daughter, wife and daughter-in-law'.

Isabella Borgia, sister of Calixtus III, had married a certain Joffré Lanzol, a nobleman of Xativa; she was the mother of several children, two of whom were boys, Roderigo and Pedro Luis. It was the boys who interested their uncle, the Pope, and he agreed to adopt them, take them under his care and supervise their careers, on condition that they abandoned their father's name of Lanzol and adopted that of their mother and himself: Borgia.

The condition was accepted and Calixtus immediately began to plan for the boys, making them his heirs. Pedro Luis, the elder, was given a position of great power when Calixtus made him not only Generalissimo of the Church, but Prefect of the City of Rome. Roderigo was started on an ecclesiastical career, became a Cardinal at the age of twenty-six, and was made Vice-Chancellor of the Church.

This caused great jealousy among other prelates and there was murmuring throughout Rome at the arrogance of the Spaniards. The Pope's countrymen were invading the country in their hundreds and securing all the best posts.

On the death of Calixtus III, the people of Rome rose in revolt against the foreigners, and one of the first to be driven from the city was Pedro Luis. He died soon afterwards.

Roderigo was more fortunately placed. He remained calm, and went to St. Peter's to pray for his uncle. His palace was

sacked by the mob, and he made no effort to save his treasures.
He appears to have been protected by his Cardinal's purple and,
no doubt, his great dignity; and even when the Pope's family
deserted his death-bed in panic, it was Roderigo who stayed
with him until the last.

At the next conclave he was able to give the decisive vote to
Aeneas Sylvius Piccolomini, who, when he became the next
Pope and reigned as Pius II, did not forget Roderigo who thus,
under his uncle's successor, resumed his old position.

When Pedro Luis died, Roderigo mourned him with a great
show of grief but the mourning was not of long duration, and
establishing himself as his brother's heir, he became one of the
richest men in Rome.

Roderigo was the more handsome of the brothers; his
manners were quite charming, but he was already betraying a
sensuality which, although he wore the robes of the Church,
he was unable to hide. He could not resist women; nor did he
see any reason why he should. It was only necessary, he
believed, to keep up a façade of virtue, and he had never used
the least restraint.

The historian Gaspare da Verona wrote of him at this time:

"He is handsome, of a most glad countenance and joyous
aspect, gifted with honeyed words and choice eloquence.
The beautiful women on whom he casts his eyes he lures to
love him and moves them in a wondrous way."

Roderigo was at this time not yet thirty years of age, and
Pope Pius took occasion to reprimand him when he wrote
complaining of an orgy at which his Cardinal had been present
and which, it seems likely, had been arranged by him.

"Dear Son," wrote Pius, "We have learned that your
Worthiness, forgetful of the high office with which you are
invested, was present from the seventeenth to the twenty-
second hour, four days ago in the gardens of Giovanni de
Bichis, where there were several women of Siena, women,
wholly given over to worldly vanities. . . ."

The letter goes on to say that none of the 'allurements of
love were lacking', and that the Cardinal's name was on every
tongue, for he had conducted himself in an unseemly and quite
worldly manner.

There is no record of how Roderigo responded to this
reprimand, but we do know that he made no attempt to change

his mode of life. He had many mistresses and the most important of these was Vannozza Cattanei.

Vannozza Cattanei was no ordinary courtesan; she must have been quite different from those women whom Roderigo would have engaged to perform the 'allurements of love' at one of the orgies which, we suspect from the letter of Pius and what we know of his later life, Roderigo indulged in from early youth to the end of his days.

We must presume that Vannozza was of great beauty. All the beauty of Rome, it seems, was ready to fall under the spell of the fascinating, wealthy and influential Cardinal Borgia; and as the children of this union were all noted for their physical beauty, it seems hardly likely that it could have come only from one side of the family.

Vannozza may have been a virtuous woman who looked upon the Cardinal as her husband, for she seems to have been faithful to him; the Cardinal later took it upon himself to arrange two marriages for her and, moreover, seemed eager to preserve her good name. She could not have been a stupid woman by any means, for the intellectual Cardinal would surely have quickly tired of her if she had been; and because of the love he bore her children, he must have looked upon her as the most important of all his mistresses. Not that the Cardinal did not love all his children; he did. But there were three on whom he doted beyond all others; they were handsome Juan, dominating Cesare and beautiful Lucrezia. And all were the children of Vannozza.

It is not certain whether the first child of this union was Juan or Cesare. According to Bellonci, Cesare was the elder; according to Gregorovius, Juan was. Gregorovius gives the dates of birth as Juan (or Giovanni) about 1474 and Cesare about 1476. There seems to be no doubt that Lucrezia was born in 1480 and Joffré (or Goffredo) in 1482.

Roderigo installed his favourite mistress in a house on the Piazza Pizzo di Merlo, which was very close to the Cardinal's palace so that he could visit her frequently and without inconvenience.

In the year 1480 when their mother was pregnant with Lucrezia the two little boys must have been already aware of their importance.

If Vannozza was a devoted mother, and I feel she must have been when the children were young, and it is known that she was devoted to Cesare all his life, she must have felt very sad at times knowing that she would not long be allowed to keep them with her. At the same time she was doubtless very proud of their beauty and intelligence, and eager that they should have all that their father was most willing to give them.

Roderigo had already several children by other mistresses. There were Girolama and Isabella, two lovely girls for whom he was eager to make not only wealthy marriages but marriages which would be useful to the Borgias. There was his son, Pedro Luis, who some authorities declare was the son of Vannozza and true brother to Cesare; but there is no proof of this.

So even when only four years old Cesare would be very much aware of his own importance. It is likely that when Roderigo visited the house he would make much of the children, bringing them presents and lavishing caresses upon them, for Roderigo was demonstrative, overflowing with sentimentality; and if his devotion was evanescent, it would seem no less sincere at the time it was displayed.

His favourite child at this time was Juan; later it might be said that Lucrezia shared the honour with her brother; but Juan was a boy, and therefore more important to the Borgia plans. There is no doubt that Cesare was also petted and admired by the father whom—at this time—he knew as uncle.

Cesare would quickly be aware that Juan was the favourite, and I have no doubt that Cesare already felt he ought to be the most important person in the nursery. It is possible that in those days he experienced the first stirrings of jealousy and hatred towards his brother, so that those seeds of enmity which were to bear tragic fruit may well have been planted in nursery days.

It was at this time that Roderigo decided that Vannozza should have a husband, for he did not forget the need to show a façade of virtue to the world. None of his fellow Cardinals would criticize him for keeping a mistress and finding places for his illegitimate children; others before him had not refrained from such human weakness; but, for the honour of the Church, it was necessary that he should put up this façade of respectability. If Vannozza were married none would think it strange that she should live contentedly surrounded by her children. The husband would be in the background for convention's sake—but in the background.

It may well have been that Vannozza herself agitated for the marriage. She was, after all, thirty-eight at the time of her pregnancy with Lucrezia, and that was well advanced into middle age for a Roman woman of that era. She might have asked herself how long she could expect to hold the interest of the Cardinal, whose virility seemed eternal.

Marriage was undoubtedly the answer, and the Cardinal agreed to provide the husband. That in itself presented no difficulty, for what man of any ambition was going to refuse to ally himself with the Borgias—particularly as, at this time, it must have been obvious that Roderigo Borgia had a fair chance of being elected Pope?

Roderigo then selected a meek man of some ambition, Giorgio di Croce, a Milanese, to be the husband of Vannozza. For his services Giorgio was made an apostolic secretary, a position Roderigo had no difficulty in obtaining from the reigning Pope Sixtus IV, who had succeeded Paul II, the successor of Pius II.

Thus the two little boys now had a 'father', but both would have realized that the important member of the household was Uncle Roderigo, who came so frequently to visit their mother and, Cesare must have readily observed, himself and his brother.

Cesare's sister Lucrezia was born on 18th April, 1480, and Uncle Roderigo was delighted with the child. He caused Roman and Spanish astrologers to cast her horoscope, and both the Romans and the Spaniards declared that an amazingly brilliant career awaited the girl.

Roderigo was making plans for his family. The times were troublous. There was war between the Vatican and Florence. The Papacy was becoming a despotic state shamelessly flaunting its nepotism, and Sixtus was accused by the Florentines of aiding a conspiracy to murder the Medici. There was little spirituality in the Papacy; power was worshipped beyond all else; and bitter feuds between families broke out suddenly and invariably ended in bloodshed.

Roderigo had seen Sixtus make a great prince of his nephew, Girolamo Riario, and he determined that what Sixtus could do for his relations, he, Roderigo, would do for his. Roderigo's plans went farther. At this time Italy was divided into several states and dukedoms which, owing to the rivalries between the rulers of these, were in a perpetual state of unrest. There were continual threats of foreign invasions. The country most feared was France, now made strong by Louis XI. France laid claim to Naples which she said was French by right of the House of Anjou; she declared that the Aragonese were usurpers. Likewise, said the French, Milan should be theirs through the House of Orléans. It may have been that, even at this time, Roderigo believed that the only strong Italy could be a united one, and that he planned to unite Italy under the rule of the Borgias.

If this union were to take place, his sons must play a big part in it, and it would be necessary for one of them to become Pope after his death, while the other must be General of the Armies. Both boys, he knew, wished to be soldiers; but clearly one must go into the Church. Roderigo made an unfortunate decision when he decided that Cesare should be the one to follow in his footsteps.

The two boys appear to have been somewhat abnormally interested in their pretty little sister. Lucrezia's pictures show her to be very attractive, although she has something less than the beauty which is often attributed to her; but her long golden hair must have been startling to a people who were mostly dark, and her light eyes equally arresting. But surely her greatest charm must have been that air of helplessness, of childishness, due to the receding chin as much as to the light wide eyes. These youthful charms stayed with her until her death. Lucrezia had the appearance of one who begged to be dominated; and perhaps this quality was responsible for the feelings she aroused in her brothers, each of whom was already beginning to feel the need to triumph over the other and show the world that he was the superior.

Perhaps it was natural that Vannozza should have made Cesare her favourite. Juan was his father's; therefore she no doubt felt the need to comfort Cesare on this account, and so grew the beginning of that devotion between them.

From the earliest days the atmosphere in that house in the Piazza Pizzo di Merlo must have been overheated with unhealthy passions.

*   *   *

During those days when the three children lived in their mother's house under the protection of the mighty Cardinal Roderigo Borgia, they must have witnessed many scenes which affected their later life and doubtless played some part in making them what they were.

If Cesare was born in 1476 he would have been eight years old when Sixtus died and there was chaos throughout Rome. The office of Pope was sought by many, and rivalry was intense. Men had seen how rich were the Popes and the Cardinals, and what honours came to their friends and relations. Therefore the election of a new Pope set hopes soaring, and determination to place a friend in the Vatican was fierce.

Innocent VIII was elected but he proved to be a quarrelsome man, and it was not long before he was at war with Naples. The powerful Orsini family, who were the allies of the

Neapolitans, caused continual trouble in Rome; at times it
was as though the city was in a state of siege. That other
powerful family, the Colonnas, perennial enemies of the
Orsinis, lost no time in attacking them. There was fierce and
bitter fighting in the streets.

The home of Vannozza was in the Ponte quarter, one of the
most heavily populated in the city since it was near the Vatican
and the Bridge of St. Angelo, so these young children would
have had a good view of sights which were terrible and degrad-
ing. They would have seen the pillaging of certain houses; the
bodies of men and women would have been mutilated before
their eyes; they would have clearly heard the cries of horror and
pain as the barbarous fighting continued. Looting and rapine
would be commonplace to them, for it must have seemed to
their young minds that this state of affairs continued for a very
long time—so long that it may have seemed normal. One
imagines the three children solemnly watching young girls—
perhaps no older than Juan and Cesare—being dragged into
the streets and publicly raped.

Did Cesare then find pleasure in such sights? It is almost
certain that he did. And Juan would have shared in that
excitement; while Lucrezia, following her brothers in all things,
would do likewise.

*   *   *

Two years after her marriage to Giorgio di Croce, Vannozza
was pregnant again. This time she gave birth to a son, Joffré. It
was natural to Roderigo that he should no longer desire his
mistress, for she was now forty and he had a particular liking for
young girls. Perhaps he realized that it would be difficult for
Giorgio to share the house of a woman like Vannozza without
sharing her bed. It is probable that one of his younger mistresses was demanding more of his attention; however Roderigo
suspected that Vannozza had committed an act of infidelity
with the husband he had provided for her, and that Joffré was
the son of Giorgio.

Roderigo showed no anger. He was grateful to Vannozza for
providing him with the delightful Juan, Cesare and Lucrezia.
Indeed he did not altogether discard Joffré, for the new baby
was enchanting—and Roderigo loved children—and showed
every sign of possessing the beauty of his brothers and sister.
All the same, on the birth of Joffré, Roderigo discontinued his
visits to Vannozza as a mistress, although it was clear that he
continued to feel the warmest regard for her.

It seems likely at this stage that the precocious Cesare and

Juan began to suspect that the magnificent and devoted
Cardinal was more to them than an uncle. They may have
discovered that they had brothers and sisters in whom their
'uncle' seemed almost as interested as he was in them. There
was Pedro Luis, a half-brother of theirs who, by the grace of
their father, had been sent to Spain where the title of Duke of
Gandia had been bestowed upon him.

One imagines the little boys in their mother's house on the
Piazza Pizzo di Merlo; it would be a somewhat dark house with
flagstone floors uncovered by rugs or carpets, and a ceiling of
beams with the wooden panelling painted. The walls would
be whitewashed, and as there would be a certain amount of
luxury in Vannozza's house, portraits probably adorned the
walls. The furniture would be heavily and elaborately carved;
there would be cushions of brilliant colours; and inevitably a
great chest to occupy a place of honour in the main room, and
which would contain the family linen. There would surely have
been, in a house enriched by the Cardinal's gifts, ornaments of
porphyry, marble and even gold. There can be no doubt that
Vannozza would have possessed the *credenza*—another great
chest in which goblets and table ornaments of silver or precious
metals would be kept, except on festive occasions—for such
things were the joy and pride of every Roman matron of
standing.

In such a house those boys must have asked themselves why
their 'uncle', who was no longer so affectionate towards their
mother, should love them as much as he ever had. They may
have asked each other who their father was. Their mother,
for all her charm and all the treasures of her house, must have
seemed to them of humble status compared with the glorious
Roderigo in his purple and jewels.

Cesare's delight to discover he was the son of the great
Cardinal must have been extreme, and limitless ambition may
have started with the discovery.

Cesare wanted to dominate all who came within his orbit.
The little Lucrezia, with her wide and innocent eyes, her
delicate charm, was an obvious victim on whom to practise his
power; and how could one of Cesare's temperament prevent
himself feeling resentment towards Juan? It may have been
that he realized that, although Roderigo was always affectionate to him, the great man's eyes would rest more often and
more lovingly on Juan. Juan would be fully aware of this and
it is unlikely that a boy of his age would be able to prevent himself from showing his triumph.

The two little boys were rivals—natural rivals. Cesare, more dominant, as handsome in his way as Juan was in his, more fierce in his determination, would feel himself to be the more deserving of success.

They must have strutted before their father, each desiring to draw attention to himself; and it may have been that Roderigo, who was far from wise in such matters, enjoyed and provoked this rivalry for his affections.

When their father was not there to be impressed, there was always their adoring sister before whom to parade their rivalry.

To all Borgias it seemed that Borgias were wonderful. None seemed as beautiful as they, none so clever. There was between them all a worship of family. Of all the girls they had ever seen neither brother had discovered one to compare in charm and beauty with Lucrezia. It was inevitable; she was a Borgia. Of all the boys Lucrezia had ever seen none had the dashing beauty of Juan or the subtle attraction, the wit of Cesare.

So in those early days of their precocious childhood in that unhealthy forcing house of passionate emotion, the two boys courted their sister, begging her favours, kissing her, embracing her, loving her. Lucrezia would have been superhuman if she could have refrained from taking advantage of this state of affairs. She did not wish to; she let them sue for her favours, always hoping that she would be able to accept Cesare as the winner.

She evidently saw in Cesare the embodiment of all masculinity, all charm. Juan too she loved. Certainly she loved him. He was handsome and a Borgia. But Cesare dominated the nursery and the house; he was the favourite of Vannozza; he was the beloved of Lucrezia; and he was determined to oust Juan from the place he held in the Cardinal's affections, and occupy it himself.

So these clever, inquisitive and precocious children played their erotic games of rivalry and conquest while still in the nursery. They looked out on the streets and saw the brutal scenes which were taking place; they came to understand why their 'uncle' visited their mother; and they began to realize that their 'uncle' was indeed their father.

They would be on the alert for gossip and they would soon discover that the Cardinals, whom they often saw riding across the bridge on their white mules, indulged in adventures such as it was their duty to deplore. They would realize that Popes did the same.

Old in knowledge, they would gravely accept this state of affairs whilst they played their games of love and passion within the family circle.

*   *.   *

Roderigo was determined to give the children Vannozza had
borne him all that lay within his power; and that power was
great. He was one of the richest men in Italy, and, as he liked
ostentation, he lived like a great prince.

Jacopo da Volterra, who was living at the time, wrote of
him that he lived in a beautiful and luxurious palace which he
had had built between the Bridge of St. Angelo and the Campo
del Fiore. His papal offices and his numerous abbeys in Italy
and Spain, together with his three Bishoprics in Valencia,
Porto and Carthage, brought him a vast income. The office
of Vice-Chancellor alone brought him eight thousand gold
florins; and he possessed plate, pearls, stuffs embroidered with
silks and gold, books of all kinds, a magnificent wardrobe, and a
great quantity of gold coins stored in his coffers. His magnificence was worthy of a king or a pope.

His interests were entirely worldly and he must have found
it very irksome that it had been necessary to attain his position
through the Church, which imposed certain restrictions. But
in spite of his promiscuity he was essentially a family man;
his devotion to his children makes that certain.

He married off his daughter Girolama to Giovanni Andrea
of the House of Cesarini, and Isabella he married to Pier-
giovanni Matuzzi; thus he allied the two powerful Houses of
Cesarini and Matuzzi with that of the Borgia, not only to the
glory of his two daughters but to the whole family.

But it was to his sons that he looked with the highest hopes;
and when news reached him of the death of Pedro Luis, for whom
he had secured the Dukedom of Gandia, he was heart-broken.
But Roderigo was by nature joyous, and found it difficult to
grieve for long, even for those whom he had sincerely loved.

He very soon stopped mourning his son Pedro Luis, and
turned with increasing affection to Vannozza's two.

Cesare was destined for the Church; therefore Juan should
go to Spain, there to take possession of his deceased brother's
estate and the bride he was to have married, as well as the
title of Duke of Gandia. Cesare should remain in Italy where
he would study canon law in Perugia and Pisa, in preparation
for his dedication to the Church.

It seems likely that at this time Cesare's jealousy of Juan
was greater than ever.

Cesare had no wish to enter the Church; but although
Roderigo was an indulgent father, he demanded obedience
from his sons; moreover at this time Cesare had not been
acknowledged as Roderigo's son, and Cesare must have been
fully aware of the necessity of obeying his benefactor.

This was probably the first frustration of any great importance in Cesare's life; and Cesare, who was born to be an extreme egoist, must have felt the first stirrings of murderous anger against a brother who had received favours from the Cardinal which he himself coveted. It must have been galling to a boy of Cesare's character to be sent to the universities of Perugia and Pisa whilst his brother was to go to Spain in great pomp and splendour.

Giorgio di Croce, to whom Vannozza had borne a son named Ottaviano, died suddenly in the year 1486; and strangely enough, little Ottaviano died the same year.

Roderigo, however, was still sufficiently interested in the welfare of the woman who had been his mistress to provide her with another husband.

This time he chose a certain Carlo Canale from Mantua. Carlo had been in the service of several Cardinals before he came to Rome, and was delighted to marry Vannozza, visualizing the advantages which would be his if he were favoured by the great Roderigo Borgia.

With Juan in Spain and Cesare at the university, Roderigo decided that he would not leave Lucrezia in the care of her mother; so he placed his beloved daughter with his cousin Adriana Mila. She was the daughter of Pedro de Mila who had come to Italy during the reign of Calixtus III when the Spaniards had arrived in their numbers looking for posts in the Vatican. She had married into the family of Orsini, and was at this time a widow with one son who had been called Orsino. Orsino Orsini was a delicate boy, a very unprepossessing one, for he had an unfortunate ailment of the eyes which made him squint.

It was while Lucrezia was living in the Orsini Palace under the care of Adriana that a marriage was arranged between Adriana's son, Orsino, and Giulia Farnese, a very beautiful young girl, admired for her long yellow hair, which was similar to that of Lucrezia.

Giulia's family, the Farnese, was an old one of nobility; but they were provincials and, although possessed of many talents, needed the opportunity to make themselves the power in the land which they felt they deserved to be. Therefore the marriage with the Orsini seemed a very good one, and the Farnese hoped that certain opportunities might come their way through it.

They were unprepared for the great good which Giulia's charm and beauty was to put in their way; for, no sooner had Roderigo set eyes on this lovely young girl than, with the passion

of a young man, he fell in love with her. Adriana, realizing
what good fortune could come to her if she connived at the
affair, did all she could to help its progress.

It is not known whether the beautiful Giulia became
Roderigo's mistress before or after her wedding to Orsino; but
there is no doubt that they were lovers. They produced living
proof in their daughter, Laura. And this was an affair smiled
on by Adriana, tolerated by the feeble Orsino, and accepted
as natural by Roderigo's children.

For Cesare and Lucrezia there could have been no surprise
at the behaviour of their father and the desire of their guardian
Adriana to pander to his lust. "Why not?" they would have
retorted if the question had been raised. "Giulia is well content."

That was true. It was clear that Giulia preferred the handsome Cardinal—in his fifties though he might be—to her poor
seventeen-year-old little husband.

Moreover her family was pleased. Had not Roderigo
bestowed the Cardinal's purple on her brother Alessandro! It
was exactly what the Farnese needed for the flowering of their
fortunes; and generations of Farnese to come would trace the
power of their House to the desire their young and lovely
daughter had aroused in the susceptible Cardinal Borgia.
Thus through the ages have families been made great.

Pope Innocent himself—pledged to a life of celibacy—was
constantly bestowing great honours on his children. Did he not
gather his children and grandchildren about him in the
Vatican?

Thus was bred in the Borgia children that indifference to
immorality and that assurance that they were chosen for
greatness.

It was brought home to them that their father was the great
Cardinal Borgia with whom such as Adriana and the Farnese
sought to ingratiate themselves.

*   *   *

Cesare distinguished himself at the University of Pisa by
his mental and physical powers. He was worldly in the extreme
and was already exhibiting such a violent antagonism towards
any who crossed him that his associates were becoming afraid
of him.

It may have been during this time that he became interested
in the use of poisons, an art which was practised in Italy more
successfully than in any other country, so that in days to come
the word Italian was to be synonymous with that of poisoner.

Cesare was beginning to see himself as one who was beyond the law. Roderigo had attracted women easily by his charm of manner, his magnificent presence, by his gentle and beguiling gift of flattery; Cesare's attractiveness was of a different kind. He is reputed to have been extremely pleasing to the eye, but it is hard to believe that he, not possessing that sentimental gentleness of Roderigo, would have used the same methods as his father to charm the women he wished to seduce.

There must have been about Cesare, even at this early stage of his career, an almost hypnotic power, which bordered on the sinister. His violent rages, his determination to dominate, may have added to this. There was clearly about Cesare, even at this time, a quality which inspired fear in his victims. To some it may have been an irresistible fear which fascinated and drew them to him while it repelled them. Could it have been that they succumbed to Cesare fearing what might happen to them if they did not?

Roderigo decided that it was time a marriage was arranged for Lucrezia, and he looked about him for suitable *partis*, young men who could bring wealth and position to Lucrezia and who would be useful in making reality of the Borgia dreams of power.

First he selected Don Cherubino Juan de Centelles who was Lord of Val d'Ayora in the Kingdom of Valencia, for Roderigo believed that marriage into a noble Spanish house was the best proposition for a daughter whom the whole world knew to be illegitimate. Arrangements were made and contracts signed. Lucrezia was to be taken to Spain where the ceremony would be performed.

But meanwhile Pope Innocent III was growing feeble, and Roderigo's desire—and indeed that of the entire family and its connections—was that Roderigo should reach the extreme pinnacle of power by being elected Pope. As Pope he would be able to make even more advantageous marriages for his children; and so he decided to annul the betrothal of Lucrezia and Cherubino in favour of one with Don Gasparo, another Spaniard, who was the son of Don Juan Francesco of Procida, Count of Aversa.

*   *   *

That event for which many ambitious Cardinals were waiting occurred in Rome. Innocent III died. There followed the fight for the succession.

The whole of Italy—the whole civilized world—waited anxiously for what would happen next.

Innocent, who died with his children at his bedside, had done little to uphold the honour of the Vatican; moreover his vacillating policy had led to trouble. He had been suspicious of the scheming men who surrounded him and who he knew were eager to take his place; he had turned to Lorenzo de' Medici for advice, which was a wise thing to have done, for it was largely due to Lorenzo that Italy had been living in peace for the last few years. But Lorenzo had died and the King of Naples, Ferrante of Aragon, and the Regent of Milan, Ludovico Sforza, were now ready to fight each other for supremacy and bring strife once more to the Italian peninsula.

So the whole country was now eager to see elected a Pope who would bring power back to the Vatican and keep the peace in Italy.

Roderigo's greatest rival to become Vicar of Christ was Giuliano della Rovere, nephew of Pope Sixtus; and before Innocent was dead, he and Roderigo were quarrelling in the sick room.

Ascanio Sforza, who was a brother of Ludovico Sforza, Regent of Milan, was another candidate behind whom were great power and the wealth which were necessary to provide the bribes which would lead to his election.

In the heat of August 1492, the Cardinals retired to their cells for the Conclave; and the first result was that Rovere had eleven votes against Roderigo's seven. Roderigo remained calm. He had come to the most important phase of his life, and the whole of Spain was watching the Conclave, determined to do a great deal to ensure that there was a Spanish Pope in the Vatican. Spain was the rising power. That year was to see its triumphant expulsion of the Moors in the completion of the conquest of Granada, the last of the Moorish strongholds. Later that year Christopher Columbus was to discover America. Spain would be the greatest power in the world, and there must be a Spanish Pope in the Vatican.

Roderigo turned his thoughts to Ascanio Sforza who, knowing himself to have no hope of being elected, would be ready, presumably, to make the best of his situation and support the candidate who could offer the best proposition with the greatest speed. Roderigo, more shrewd than Rovere, promised Sforza the Vice-Chancellorship, the Borgia Palace and the Bishopric of Nepi—which was a very wealthy one—if in exchange for this bounty, Sforza would bring the support of the Milanese party to Roderigo.

Sforza saw the advantages of the offer and agreed.

Crowds assembled in St. Peter's Square waiting for the

news while other candidates and men of power, realizing the action of the Milanese, hastened to the support of Roderigo who had made it clear that the bribes he would offer to those who supported him would surpass any of those given by his predecessors.

The silver mallet struck against the walled-up window and the proclamation was made to all those waiting below: Roderigo Borgia, Cardinal of Valencia and Vice-Chancellor of the Church, Bishop of Oporto and Abbot of Subiaco, was now elected Pope and from henceforth would be known as Alexander VI.

The new Pope showed himself on the balcony and cried out with great joy: "I am Pope and Vicar of Christ on Earth."

Thus at the age of sixty Roderigo, through his shrewdness and cunning, had reached his goal. He had waited over thirty years for this day. His triumph must have seemed complete and his head was filled with grandiose plans for the advancement of his family.

*   *   *

The coronation took place on 26th August, 1492, and was one of the most magnificent spectacles seen in Rome for many years. People had crowded into the city which had been lavishly decorated for the occasion, and everywhere could be seen the emblem of a grazing bull, which was the Borgia arms; comfits in the shape of bulls were offered for sale; and in St. Mark's Square the new Pope Alexander had had an enormous gilded bull erected and from the horns of this animal wine poured, that the thirsty sightseers might drink the health of Alexander VI while they slaked their thirst.

The Tiber was full of craft of all descriptions, and there were not enough lodgings to be found for all the visitors to the city, so that many were forced to encamp in the streets.

There was no fighting on that day. The two great families between whom a perpetual vendetta seemed to exist—the Orsinis and the Colonnas—forgot their quarrels and added to the splendour of the procession.

Alexander must have been elated. He enjoyed spectacles, and what could be more delightful than to be the central figure in such a splendid one. Seven hundred priests and cardinals, all with their retinues, the archers and Turkish horsemen, the guards of the palace holding their shimmering lances and shields, made a dazzling show.

But the greatest moment for the spectators was that when the

Pope himself appeared. Serene, dignified, he was the handsomest Pope that had ever been seen. His beautiful features
were composed, never betraying for an instant the triumph
he must have felt over his rivals, accepting the homage of all
as his due. He sat his snow-white horse like a god and the
people wept with joy to see him.

So long was the procession that it took two hours to pass
from St. Peter's to St. John Lateran. The heat was intense, yet
during all that time the sixty-year-old Pope Alexander sat his
horse, smiling benignly, deeply content, now that all he had
hoped for had come to pass.

Spain was triumphant at home and in Rome.

*   *   *

Cesare would have been about sixteen at the time of his
father's coronation, but he was immediately made Archbishop
of Valencia. Alexander, however, did not call his son home to
Rome immediately. He did not wish to show nepotism too
blatantly, and he hoped to hide his indulgence in this practice
by keeping his son from appearing in too much state at the
beginning of his reign.

However, Spaniards were now filling the best posts at the
Vatican; Alexander was looking after his relations, and it
was said that ten papacies would not have been enough to
satisfy them all.

Now that he was Pope, Alexander began to think again
about Lucrezia's marriage. It no longer seemed to him that
the limit of his ambition for her need be a Spanish nobleman.
So he looked for a prince and his eyes alighted on Giovanni
Sforza who was Count of Cotignola and Vicar of Pesaro;
although these titles were not great ones Giovanni was an
independent sovereign and a scion of the famous house of
Sforza. Such a marriage would bring to the Vatican the firm
support of Ludovico the Regent of Milan, and Ascanio Sforza.

Alexander then annulled the betrothal with Don Gasparo,
for Giovanni Sforza did not hesitate a moment, realizing the
importance of an alliance with the powerful Borgia.

*   *   *

Alexander VI did not wish to keep his beloved son Cesare
from his presence for too long a time, and it was soon after
the coronation that Cesare returned to Rome.

Cesare was making it clear that he had no love for the
calling which had been chosen for him. His dress was quite
worldly and he rode about the city fully armed; he wore only

a little tonsure as a simple priest would, and he was arrogant.
Surrounded by favourites of both sexes, he was more determined than ever to dominate all who came within his reach, not
excluding his father.

He could be charming, but the sinister streak in his nature
was ever present, and apparent. Few dared cross him. Although
he did not yet feel himself to be completely frustrated—and it
was when he felt this frustration that he became dangerous—
he had already lived the life of a dissolute student, arranging
orgies to satisfy his own peculiar taste and that of those who
dared do no other than follow him.

At this time he must have believed in his power to persuade
his father to bring about his release from the Church.

When he returned to Rome he lived in the Borgo, close to
his sister's home. He visited her frequently and Lucrezia felt
the power of that spell which he had always cast over her.
It is said that Cesare loved two people only—his mother
Vannozza and his sister Lucrezia. It may have been that
Cesare loved these two because they gave him that unquestioning devotion and submission which he sought from the rest of
the world.

When he returned to find Lucrezia betrothed to Sforza he
was jealous, since he could not endure contemplating his sister
with a lover. His inability to stop the marriage was the beginning of frustration. Cesare wanted power, not only over those
whom he had gathered about him during his university career
when he had started to make a little court of his own, but over
everyone—sister, brother and father.

Cesare was to grow almost insane with egoism. Determined
to be head of his family, did he at this time begin to formulate
plans for uniting and ruling Italy? Young as he was he had
already learned how to inspire fear in almost everyone with
whom he came into contact; and he was beginning to believe
that he might inspire that fear even in the great Pope, his
father.

He had enormous energy, and he must find outlets for it.
A great deal of it was expended in violent rages which possessed
him at times; then he would invent tortures for those who
offended him. But he quickly tired of the scenes he caused to
be enacted before his eyes, and must continually invent newer
and wilder entertainment.

Here he was then, believing himself capable of uniting and
ruling Italy, forced into the Church when it was his ambition
to be a soldier, to lead men in battle, to fight and win, to enter
vanquished cities and leave behind him a trail of rape and

murder, fire and torture, such as had never been known before, so that the name of Cesare Borgia should be dreaded by all men and the whole world tremble before him.

There was only one way he knew as yet in which to defy these people who would seek to obstruct him in what he wished to do. He made no effort to act like a man of the Church. Although Popes and Cardinals had had their mistresses and swarms of illegitimate children, even living at the Vatican, they had at least made some effort to hide these facts when necessary to decorum. So Cesare showed his defiance by dressing as a layman, by riding through the streets of Rome in the company of his mistresses, of whom there was one, a red-haired Florentine named Fiametta who was an accomplished courtesan.

This was scandalous enough; but there was another rumour in the streets of Rome. Cesare was often seen in the company of his sister; he was observed visiting her. They openly behaved like lovers, and there were spies to report that they spent nights together. It was said that Cesare Borgia was determined that his sister should be his mistress before she was the bride of any other.

Cesare without doubt was the most important person in Lucrezia's life at this time, as he probably was until his death. Cesare set the pace and Lucrezia followed.

But for all the fear he inspired and for all the rumours, he could not escape from the Church, nor could he prevent the marriage of his sister to Giovanni Sforza. Alexander was Pope, father, and head of the family; and Alexander had decided that Cesare should walk in his footsteps and that Lucrezia should ally the powerful Sforzas to the House of Borgia.

*　　　*　　　*

On a hot June day Lucrezia wearing a gold-embroidered dress which cost fifteen thousand ducats, her golden hair caught in a jewelled net, was married to Giovanni Sforza.

Juan had come home from Spain, and it was he who led his sister to the Pope's apartments where the ceremony was to take place.

Cesare was present, his resentment suppressed. In his episcopal garments he would have made a striking contrast to Juan, dazzling with his jewels. He would have resented not only his brother but the bridegroom who was to marry his sister.

Lucrezia looked essentially virginal; her somewhat blank expression was that of a wide-eyed child; and it was small wonder that, when it was declared she was too young for the consummation of the marriage, this was agreed to be so.

Juan looked very handsome in his jewelled garments, and Lucrezia, ever ready to be enamoured of the members of her own family, may have wondered whether she was now going to play once more that game of creating jealousy and passion which she had enjoyed with her brothers when she was a small girl.

In the apartment decorated with the first of Pinturicchio's landscapes, with its gold ceiling, marble brackets, silk and velvet hangings and oriental carpets, Lucrezia was married to Sforza. It was all brilliance and splendour and Alexander looked on with benevolent satisfaction.

At the supper party which followed in the Pope's apartment, Cesare was not present; and as he was the only member of the family to absent himself, it is very likely that he did so in his jealous rage at seeing his sister married to another man.

Lucrezia seemed placidly to have accepted his absence as she did so many things in her life. Juan was very handsome in his Turkish costume cut in the French manner, so long that it swept the floor; it would have been quite dazzling, for it was made of cloth of gold and great pearls were sewn into the sleeves. The collar of this garment was of rubies and pearls; and he wore a cap which was adorned with one solitary gem of almost blinding magnificence.

There is an account of how Lucrezia and Juan together danced the old Spanish dances which they had learned in their childhood, and that, when she danced thus with Juan, a creature of fire and passion emerged from that quiet girl who was not considered old enough to consummate the marriage.

The Pope looked on with pleasure to see the children on whom he doted dancing thus together; he laughed with great heartiness at the sly jokes and bawdy songs which would seem to him a natural part of the wedding celebrations. He might have thought that perhaps it was as well that Cesare was not present. Cesare's anger would have been inflamed to see Lucrezia and Juan thus together.

After the celebration Lucrezia was conducted to her apartments by her attendants, and Giovanni Sforza was left to his own devices, for he must remember that clause in the marriage treaty which declared Madonna Lucrezia not yet of a marriageable age.

*   *   *

Lucrezia turned from one brother to the other, finding them both delightful—as her husband never could be.

Cesare had decided that the bridegroom was beneath his

notice, and his mind was obsessed by his hatred of other
enemies: Juan and the Farnese family.

Cesare had always seen himself as of the utmost significance;
other people were only considered according to the part they
played in his life; those who pleased him, he charmed; those
who displeased him, he sought to remove.

People without power behind them could disappear suddenly, and no questions would be asked. Cesare had his band of
assassins, and any who defied him must either escape from his
venom or it might be that one day they would be set upon by
ruffians in the street, stabbed and left to die; some might be
tied in sacks and thrown into the Tiber.

There was another method of disposing of enemies and this
was by poison. Cesare found this a more satisfying method
than any other. It could be easily administered at his table;
he himself could watch its being done. He could lift his goblet,
drink with a man, and know that before the night was over
that man would be dead. The sense of power such action
brought to him was an intoxication.

Many secret poisons were known to him, for they had been
brought to Spain by the Moors; these secrets had been pre-
served for centuries and were known only to his family.
Cesare craved power, power over his fellow men and women,
power over life and death.

Thus it was that people who offended Cesare died mysteriously. It seemed to many, who did not know his secrets, that
Cesare had but to look and that look sufficed to kill.

Now, had his hatred been directed at any others but his
brother and the Farnese, Cesare would not have hesitated to
use the dagger or poison. But Giulia Farnese was still the most
important of Alexander's mistresses, and Cesare knew that at
present he was in no position to arouse his father's wrath.
Juan was his father's beloved son, and Cesare knew that the
Pope loved all his children with a deep passion and a desire for
their advancement; yet much as he doted on Cesare, Juan
remained his favourite.

There was nothing Cesare could do at that time but curb his
jealous anger; and the suppressing of Cesare's anger always
made it burn the more fiercely.

Alexander was going ahead with his plans for his family.

Little Joffré, now about eleven, was betrothed to Sanchia of
Aragon who was sixteen years old. Sanchia was the natural
daughter of Alfonso, heir to the throne, and the marriage
was calculated to strengthen the alliance between the Vatican
and Naples.

The betrothal ceremony took place in the Pope's apartments with the Prince Federico representing Sanchia. This gave rise to much ribaldry, for Federico mimed the part of a reluctant virgin, and the solemn ceremony became as a frivolous masque. This was considered particularly amusing as Sanchia's reputation had travelled before her, and it was said that she had already entertained a host of lovers.

The Pope was hilariously gay on this occasion. It seemed to him a great joke that this experienced young woman of sixteen should be the bride of his eleven-year-old Joffré, who was enchantingly pretty, but as a girl is pretty.

Alexander loved little Joffré as he loved all his children, even though he was not sure whether Joffré was his son or not. As far as that was concerned, he made excuses for Vannozza. She was such an attractive and fruitful woman.

His children were a great blessing to him, and he was delighted to have Juan home. The sojourn in Spain had improved Juan in his father's eyes. Juan was handsome—the handsomest of his sons—and both of them, Juan and Cesare, were continually bringing charming people whom they had discovered, to minister to their father's pleasure. They shared these visitors, if they were girls. (The Pope, unlike his sons, had never been attracted by beautiful young men.) But it was a great pleasure for Alexander to share these experiences, and if he could be sure that Cesare would reconcile himself to his fate, the Pope would feel himself indeed blessed in his family.

* * *

It was necessary to enforce discipline. Juan, after his stay in Rome, had no wish to leave the city; but his father insisted that he must claim his dukedom and get himself an heir; and for that reason, much as it grieved Alexander to part from his favourite son, Juan was forced to return to Spain.

Before Juan left, Alexander assured him that there were certain rules which he must insist on his obeying. He must conform with Spanish customs and be a good husband, by which he meant Juan must not fail to keep his wife company at night until the desired result had been achieved.

Juan, however, was determined to have his own way. He quickly squandered the fortune which his father had given him and, disliking his not very beautiful Spanish bride, refused to consummate the marriage.

Alexander then found it necessary to be very stern. He issued orders to Juan—and like Cesare, Juan knew that there were times when the Pope's instructions must be obeyed to the letter—with the result that Juan was soon able to report that his wife expected a child.

* * *

Juan's expectations, Cesare would realize, meant the end of his own hopes of escape from the Church. If Juan had failed to beget an heir, then the Pope might have felt it was necessary to release Cesare from bondage that he might attempt to provide the Borgias with heirs. Alas for Cesare, that hope was lost.

He must have raged against his father's decision. He knew that he was as unsuitable for the Church as Juan was to become the leader of the Pope's armies. This frustration, suppressed, smouldering, soured his character. He had been ruthless and determined to dominate before he knew this frustration; now it burst out in acts of studied cruelty.

He could not use this against the people who angered him: his father, his brother, and the Farnese family who, he saw, were becoming more and more powerful through Giulia's influence over the Pope. Therefore he turned it against his servants and all others over whom he had the slightest power.

He craved self-aggrandizement; he wanted all the world to see him as he saw himself; not as a man of the Church, but as a great conqueror, the most powerful man in Rome.

When his father decided that it was time he became a Cardinal, he must have felt escape from the Church would never be achieved.

Alexander was determined to override all the difficulties which stood in his way of bestowing the purple on Cesare; and even this brought humiliation to his proud son.

The ancient law did not allow a bastard to become a Cardinal.

But Alexander was not going to allow such a law however ancient to stand in the way of what he wanted, so he set about legitimizing his son. Cesare was therefore described as the son of Vannozza and a Bishop; but Vannozza, so it was said, was a married woman at the time, and a child of a married woman was, in law, the child of her husband. Vannozza's husband (according to Infessura) had been Domenico d'Arignano, a man who was employed by the Church; therefore Cesare was not, in law, illegitimate, and could be elected to the Sacred College.

The Pope had allowed Cesare to adopt the name of Borgia because he was benevolent, interested in the family and was determined to help the sons in their careers.

At the same time Alexander could not bear to disown any of

his beloved children—after all, he was very proud of them—
so he signed another Bull, which he kept secret, declaring that
he was indeed the father of Cesare.

Many historians referring to these Bulls bring forward the
information therein as proof that Cesare was the elder of the two
brothers. Alexander implies in these Bulls that after the death
of Domenico d'Arignano, another son was born to Vannozza
and this son was Juan. Therefore, it would seem that Cesare was
the elder, since he was supposed to have been born during the
lifetime of d'Arignano.

This may be so, but, on the other hand, as this matter was
raised purely that Cesare might be proved legitimate and so be
allowed to become a Cardinal, the information may arouse
suspicions in some minds, and the birth dates of the brothers
remain uncertain.

Alexander knew that there was going to be a great deal of
opposition to the election of Cesare, and as he had promised
Giulia that her brother Alessandro should have a Cardinal's
hat, and he guessed that the election of his mistress's brother
would be as unpopular as that of Cesare, he was prepared for
storms.

He chose an opportunity when the sultry weather had
brought a threat of plague to the City so that many of the
Cardinals had left for the country, when he called together
a Consistory. Less than half the Cardinals were able to attend.
He then produced a list of new Cardinals for the approval of
the College of Cardinals, and at the head of this list was his son
Cesare and the brother of his mistress, Alessandro Farnese.

Unfortunately for Alexander his old enemy and rival della
Rovere, had not left Rome, and this energetic man was able to
rouse his fellow Cardinals to fury over this blatant favouritism.
The question of the wisdom of holding the election at such a
time, when so many of their number were absent, was raised.
Alexander was asked if he had given due consideration to the
matter. There was a threat behind these words and Alexander
must have been aware of the pleasure of his old enemy in his
discomfiture.

But Alexander was a man of great resource and courage. He
determined to quash rebellion before it had time to grow. He
was certainly not going to withdraw Cesare and Alessandro
from the list. He rose in his wrath and in a short speech made
them understand that he, who was so ready to be charming and
gay and overlook their venial sins, demanded absolute obedience, and warned them that if any opposed a Borgia Pope they
would regret it.

That group of Cardinals—and their families—may have remembered rumours they had heard of Borgia methods of disposing of their enemies. Cesare's reputation as a poisoner was well known, but from whom had Cesare learned his secrets? If it were true that the obscure Borgia methods were derived from the Spanish Moors, Cesare must have learned of these matters from his father.

Della Rovere discreetly left Rome, and Cesare and Alessandro Farnese became Cardinals.

*　　　*　　　*

Cesare was moving towards the climax of jealousy and frustration. Now that Juan was away, his jealousy of his sister's husband was growing to a madness.

Giovanni Sforza was becoming very uneasy. Ascanio Sforza, his kinsman, had opposed the election of the new Cardinals and thus had brought down the wrath of the Pope on his head. This had resulted in a great loss of power for Ascanio Sforza, and Giovanni, as his relation, suffered accordingly.

He knew that the Pope looked with disfavour on his family and he knew also that Cesare hated him.

He must continually watch what he ate and drank.

None knew the components of that subtle draught which the Borgias were apt to slip into the wine of those they considered to be their enemies. All were sure that it could provide death in some form or another. Some men, after partaking of it, appeared to go into a drunken sleep from which they did not wake; others went merrily away to be seized by violent agony during the night and die before the dawn broke; some contracted a lingering illness which did not affect them until weeks later. They went into declines; their hair fell out; their nails dropped off, and their teeth broke as though they had suddenly become as brittle as glass.

And all were sure that these deaths were brought about by the mysterious concoctions of the Borgias.

If one were threatened, thought Giovanni, there was only one thing a wise man could do: slip away out of their reach.

This was what he did. One night he went out as though to visit a friend and did not return.

Lucrezia was indifferent to the loss of her husband. She had tolerated him in her palace, but she had cared nothing for him; her brothers had made sure of that.

Alexander however was disturbed by his son-in-law's flight and began agitating for his return, holding out as a bait the consummation of the marriage.

When Giovanni refused to come back to Rome, Alexander decided that Lucrezia must go to him, and so she set out for her husband's domain of Pesaro.

Away from her family in beautiful Pesaro—situated in a valley surrounded by hills, faced by the sea and dominated by the two mountains, Accio and Ardizio, and watered by the Foglia River—Lucrezia was made much of by the people and entertained by the festivities arranged to welcome her; Lucrezia was content to stay awhile.

* * *

In September of the year 1494, Charles VIII of France invaded Piedmont. His fleet had defeated that of the Aragonese at Rapallo, and the Army began marching on towards Naples, passing triumphantly on through Pisa. There Girolamo Savonarola, the reformer, who was preaching against the wickedness into which the Church had fallen, met the French King and declared he saw in him God's agent who had come to reform the Church.

The French reached Florence and prepared for the onslaught on Rome.

Meanwhile Giulia and her sister who were travelling with Adriana were captured by French soldiers and held to ransom. Alexander seemed more grieved concerning the fate of his mistress than that of Rome. When the French demanded a price of 3,000 scudi he hastened to provide it and was in a state of frantic anxiety until he heard that the ladies had been freed. It was fortunate that the little party had fallen into the hands of a certain French commander named Yves d'Allegre who had high ideals of chivalry; these were shared by his men, and the ladies were unharmed.

When Alexander heard that his mistress and her companions were on their way to Rome he behaved like a young lover. He seemed to forget that Rome was in imminent danger. He dressed himself in a black velvet cloak which was trimmed with cloth of gold, Spanish scarf, velvet jewelled cap and Valencia boots, and prepared to greet them.

The whole of Italy was talking about the Pope's passion for this young girl, the devotion he displayed towards their little daughter Laura, and the scandal he was bringing to the Vatican. Alexander cared nothing for rumours. He did not believe in failure. He knew that he was in great danger, but it did not occur to him for a moment that he would not be able to extricate himself from that danger.

He ordered that trunks be filled with his treasures and

prepared to retreat, but news came that Civitavecchia had fallen
to the French; therefore escape by boat was cut off. He retired
to that fortress which he believed to be impregnable: Castel
Saint Angelo.

The French entered Rome, and from his fortress the Pope
could see the signs of their occupation. There had been no
resistance and the armies of Charles had marched triumphantly in, bearing with them the fruits of conquest—magnificent
cloth and dazzling jewels, the treasures of Florence. Then
began the rape of Rome. Houses were plundered; women were
raped; and in Castel Saint Angelo Alexander would be fully
aware of this, so he set his astute mind to work out some means
of throwing off the invader.

He began negotiations with the French; he agreed to give
them right of transit through the Papal States. To show his
good faith he offered to hand over as a hostage to the French
his beloved son, Cesare.

He received Charles in the Vatican, to which he had now
returned, and charmed the French King, who agreed to leave
Rome, taking Cesare with him.

Cesare must have enjoyed this escapade. It brought him into
the limelight; he may have hoped that it proved to his father
and the people of Italy that he was worthy to lead them against
the French, that his abilities were more suited to the strategy
of battle than to the Church.

He rode beside the King down the Appian Way, and the
French were amused by the foppish Cardinal who had brought
with him seventeen wagons, all covered in velvet, containing
his clothes and all that he would need for a journey. But
Cesare showed them that they had been mistaken if they
thought him a fop, for when the French indulged in a favourite
pastime of wrestling, Cesare stripped to the waist and joined in
the fun. He acquitted himself well, which made the French
more respectful than they had been at the beginning of the
journey.

The cavalcade rested at Velletri near the Pontine Marshes
and settled down for the night. With the dawn it was realized
that Cesare was missing. He had left the camp and found his
way to an inn where he had arranged that a servant should be
waiting with horses. As for the seventeen velvet-covered wagons,
he had had no compunction in leaving them in the hands of
the French, for when they were examined they were found to
contain nothing at all.

When news was brought to Alexander of his son's escape he
shook his head sadly and said that the Cardinal had behaved

very badly; but in private he laughed aloud, and it was clear that he thought his son Cesare was a very fine fellow indeed.

The French could do nothing but push on. Naples offered no resistance, and there they rested to recuperate after the long march south.

Alexander was busy. He made an alliance with Venice, Naples, the Emperor Maximilian and the King of Spain, all of whom were determined not to see Italy fall under French domination.

Charles, resting in Naples, saw that for him the position had rapidly deteriorated. He realized that there was only one course open to him and that was return to France.

He decided to leave a small force in Naples, and before he left Italy he was determined to see the Pope, who he considered had treated him treacherously.

Alexander however had no intention of seeing the French King. There would be recriminations and he hated unpleasantness, so before Charles reached Rome Alexander retired to Perugia.

Here he lived in state, and deciding that he could no longer bear to be separated from his beloved daughter, he demanded that her husband restore her to her family, declaring that if Giovanni Sforza did not obey the Pope's wishes he should be excommunicated.

Sforza brought Lucrezia to Perugia.

Cesare was also with his father at Perugia. Cesare was delighted to be with his sister, as she was to see him. The year she had spent in Pesaro would then have seemed a wasted year, although it was characteristic of Lucrezia that she should not be aware of this at the time. Lucrezia, at this phase of her life, seemed colourless, wishing only to be dominated. Cesare and her father were very willing to do the dominating. Sforza, serious and cold, unable to enjoy the ribald jokes which were understood in the Borgia family, must have seemed infinitely boring when compared with the gay and charming Alexander and the fascinating, unaccountable Cesare.

Spending his time between prayer and erotic living, Alexander enjoyed his stay at Perugia.

Cesare was growing more sullen and discontented with his Cardinal's robes; he was apt to fly into sudden rages and because he kept these under some control, they seemed no less alarming, for those who witnessed them knew that Cesare was aware to what lengths his anger could carry him. Lucrezia would have noticed the change in Cesare. She would have heard of the torture he had inflicted on Swiss soldiers who had

looted his mother's house at the time of the French invasion.
Cesare would consider this violation of his mother's property
as a slur on the Borgias; his pride was great. He was determined that none should slight it and live, and that the death
those soldiers suffered for the desecration should not be an easy
one.

Alexander soon tired of Perugia and, as there was no reason
why he should not now return to Rome, he did so, taking his
beloved children with him.

*   *   *

During the trouble with the French, disturbing stories had
reached Alexander of his daughter-in-law, Sanchia. He had
contemplated sending for her to come to Rome, although the
terms of the marriage treaty between her and Joffré were that
they should live in Naples. The French invasion had caused
him to put all thoughts of Sanchia from his mind, but now he
was thinking of her once more.

Sanchia, he heard, was one of the most beautiful women
in the world. She was also one of the most immoral; she was so
skilled in the arts of love and luring men to her that she was
suspected of witchcraft, for it was said that none could have
such power unless it was supernatural. She took advantage of
her married state and her very young bridegroom to lead her
own fantastically licentious life.

Alexander let it be known that he could no longer turn a
blind eye and a deaf ear to such conduct in the family, but
secretly he was contemplating with relish the thought of having
such an exciting relative in the immediate family circle.

When the French had invaded Naples, Sanchia's father had
been forced to abdicate, and had lost his senses. The Court went
into exile. But now the French had been driven out order was
restored to Naples. Back in the Vatican, Alexander sent orders
that his son Joffré and his bride Sanchia were to come to
Rome.

Rome eagerly awaited their coming, for the rumours concerning Sanchia had spread throughout the whole length and
breadth of Italy.

Cesare as eagerly awaited the arrival of Sanchia. Lucrezia
was a little apprehensive. If Sanchia was as beautiful and as
irresistible as she was made out to be, Lucrezia feared that
Cesare might be interested in the newcomer.

Joffré and Sanchia arrived on a brilliant May day in the
year 1496.

It was a dazzling procession which marched up the Appian

Way with the sun shining on the jewels and bright costumes of
attendants, ladies, gentlemen, pages, jesters and soldiers. In
the midst of this splendour rode the young couple, dressed—in
contrast with their brightly clad attendants—in traditional
Spanish black. Joffré, like all Alexander's children, was
arrestingly attractive to the eye. His features were as delicate
as a girl's, and had his curls been golden, instead of auburn,
he would have looked very like his sister Lucrezia.

Sanchia rode beside him, painted and elegant in a black,
embroidered, wide-sleeved gown, which was wholly Spanish in
style. There was no doubt of Sanchia's extraordinary beauty,
and it was agreed that in comparison Lucrezia looked insipid.

Lucrezia had ridden out to meet her sister-in-law accompanied by twelve beautiful girls, charmingly dressed, and
two pages whose gold and red costumes looked splendid indeed.
Lucrezia in green and gold brocade and feathered hat looked
delicately beautiful, but she was outshone by Sanchia, Princess
of Squillace, and she knew that she had been right to fear her
as a rival.

Sanchia was dark-haired and dark-skinned, but her eyes
were startlingly blue; and her lashes and brows were as black
as her hair. Her mouth was full and sensuous; and in contrast
with Lucrezia's look of girlish innocence, Sanchia had a look
of witchery and deep knowledge.

The people of Rome, watching this nineteen-year-old girl,
prophesied that she would bring trouble to the Vatican.

They were right. Sanchia immediately set about charming
those two whom she sensed to be the most important people in
the Vatican—the Pope and Cesare.

The Pope was soon under her spell, and permitted her to
flout Vatican etiquette so persistently that this was soon the
cause of scandal among the Cardinals. As for Cesare, he
immediately began plans for the seduction of his brother's wife.

Sanchia had heard of Cesare's reputation, and was fascinated by that most dangerous man in Rome. She realized the
need to accept him as a lover, for to have repulsed Cesare might
have meant to endanger her life. She was too careless and
impulsive to watch what *she* ate and drank; therefore she told
herself that submission to Cesare would be not only a pleasure
but a necessity. This prince of vice must certainly have whetted
her appetite. It would be amusing to discover who was the
more knowledgeable in pleasures of the senses.

Joffré, only too glad to have the attentions of his insatiable
wife turned from himself, welcomed Cesare to their apartments; and very soon Lucrezia joined them there.

It was said in Rome that Lucrezia looked with acute jealousy on her brother's courtship of Sanchia, and became Sanchia's constant companion, not out of love for her sister-in-law but because, by frequenting Sanchia's apartments, she was likely to meet Cesare there.

When Lucrezia left Rome for Pesaro once more in the company of her husband, there were many to suggest that she went willingly because the perpetual sight of her brother and Sanchia together made her so jealous that she was unable to endure her life.

Cesare did not love Sanchia any more than Sanchia loved Cesare. They were two sensual people who recognized in each other an equal sensuality. Neither had ever curbed his or her desire; each was full of knowledge in these matters and enjoyed imparting it to the other. It seems that their relationship was one of rivalry rather than one of affection.

Cesare felt differently about Lucrezia. When Lucrezia married he had been filled with anger to contemplate her with a husband, but he did not care how many lovers Sanchia took. They flaunted their sexual prowess, vying with each other in their excesses; there was no love, not even a mild affection.

*   *   *

Juan returned to Rome, leaving his wife and son in Spain. All Cesare's jealousy returned, for no sooner was his favourite installed at the Vatican than Alexander began to consider what new honours he could give to this young man. Cesare, smouldering with jealousy, hating the robes of the Church which he was forced to wear, let his rage against his brother grow into a murderous frenzy. This was not alleviated in any way when Juan—who was as vicious and promiscuous as Cesare—cast his eyes on Sanchia. Juan was very handsome and Sanchia could never resist any man who attracted her; so it was not long before it was said in Rome that Sanchia of Aragon 'warmed the beds of the Pope's three sons'.

Cesare, seeing himself twice the stature of ordinary men would, had Juan been anyone but his brother, have soon arranged that he should come into contact with the assassin's knife or sip the poison cup. But the fount of all their glory was Alexander, and while loving all his children devotedly, Alexander continued to favour Juan. Cesare, therefore, was forced to watch falling to Juan all for which he himself longed; and, as his love for members of his own family was greater than that which he could feel for any others, so was his hate.

*   *   *

For long Alexander had planned an attack on the Orsini. During the French invasion they had gone over to the enemy and allied themselves with the invader; this was unforgivable and Alexander no doubt felt that small states should be taught that they could not act in this manner with impunity. It is thought that Alexander's plan was to found a Borgia dynasty, and this he would do by eliminating petty rulers; it is suggested that his flagrant nepotism had something more behind it than benevolence towards his own family, and that it was part of this plan to make the Borgias powerful throughout Italy.

Now seemed the time to launch an experimental attack on the Orsini, because Virginio Orsini, the leader of the clan, was at this time being held prisoner in Naples.

Moreover here was Juan, thirsting for military glory. Cesare also thirsted, but Alexander would not be turned from his determination that Cesare should follow him to the Papacy.

So Juan was given command of the Pope's armies while Cesare remained in Rome, cursing his fate. Juan was not successful as a military commander, and Cesare must have laughed with vicious delight at his brother's failure, for Juan was bringing the Pope's armies into ridicule; and at length it was necessary for Alexander to make peace with his enemies.

Alexander was clever; he knew that although his enemies were victorious they were in no mood to continue fighting. A diplomatist of the first order, he secured the best possible terms so that it might seem that the Pope was the victor.

It was impossible, however, to keep Virginio Orsini a prisoner any longer, for that was something the Orsinis would not tolerate. Alexander had to agree to his release, but he was anxious. He knew that it was inevitable that, once free and returned to his estate, Virginio would plot his revenge against the Pope. Something had to be done to prevent this.

Alexander was not by nature a poisoner, and it may have been that on this occasion he called in the help of his son Cesare. Cesare, half Italian, was devoted to the art already. Therefore it would seem to him a simple matter to prevent Virginio's plotting against them.

Virginio, by seeming coincidence, died on the very day he was—in accordance with the peace terms—to be released from his prison.

His timely death caused a certain amount of rumour. Previously it was those in Cesare's immediate circle who had whispered of his ways with his enemies; now all Italy marvelled at the skill of the Borgias who could condemn a man to death, though he were miles away from them, and make that death

seem a natural one, apart from the fact that it was so convenient to the Borgias.

*   *   *

With Juan humiliated, and Sanchia his mistress, Cesare
began to think longingly of Lucrezia, for it maddened him
to think of his beloved sister as the wife of such a man as
Giovanni Sforza. The Pope agreed with Cesare that, in view of
the changing political scene, the continuation of the marriage
could bring no good to the Borgias. It might be advisable to
recall the pair to Rome. Perhaps Cesare suggested this; it may
have been that after the death of Virginio, Cesare began to
exercise his power over Alexander. There is no doubt that he
wielded this later and the murder could have brought them
closer together. However, it was decided that their beloved
Lucrezia must be rid of such a burden. But how? Divorce was
disgraceful, and the Vatican must frown on it. Perhaps other
means could be used for the disposal of Sforza—other more
discreet and less scandalous methods such as those to which
Cesare was very ready to introduce his father?

So back to Rome came Lucrezia and her husband.

Lucrezia was less determinedly vicious than her brother;
she was in fact more like her father. Lucrezia drifted listlessly
into vice, and one feels that most certainly, in a different
environment, she would, at any rate, in her early youth, have
been a rather colourless character.

She was by no means in love with her frigid husband. It was
clear that she found him a very poor substitute for Cesare as a
lover; and the thought of being rid of him would have aroused
no great distress; but she knew her family and she knew the
way in which their minds were working; and Lucrezia was
afraid for Sforza. Unexciting as he had been, she did not care
to contemplate his death agonies in some dark alley, nor the
violent and horrible contortions which might follow his eating
of some dish or drinking wine prepared for him; she did not
wish to watch him under the effect of some slow-working
poison with which Cesare was so devilishly clever, and which
weeks, or perhaps months, after the poison had been administered, ended in the gradual atrophy and dropping off of the
limbs.

Many authorities believe that when Lucrezia returned to
Rome and understood what her father and brother were
plotting, she determined to save her husband. Lucrezia was in
a quandary; how could she warn Sforza against her beloved
Cesare? That would be tantamount to disloyalty to the person

she loved devotedly and beyond all others. Yet how could she stand aside and see her husband murdered? The story goes that one day when she knew Cesare was going to visit her and discuss the plans he was making for the removal of her husband, she arranged that Jacomino, her husband's chamberlain whom she knew to be completely faithful to him, should be in her apartments. Warning Jacomino that her brother was on his way to see her and that if he discovered the chamberlain in the privacy of her apartments he would be furiously angry, she hid Jacomino behind the hangings. Thus when Cesare discussed the plans he had made for the murder of Sforza, Jacomino heard all, and afterwards made with all speed to his master to warn him.

Sforza, considering the reputation of his enemies, decided that he should depart with all speed.

He announced that he was going to church—this occurred during Holy Week—and set out for St. Onofrio. There he found, as he had arranged, a horse waiting for him. It was a strong Turkish horse, but he rode with such speed to Pesaro that when he reached his own domain, the horse dropped dead beneath him.

*   *   *

It was now realized in the Vatican that the more scandalous method of releasing Lucrezia must be employed: Divorce.

It was therefore announced that the marriage between Lucrezia and Sforza had never been consummated and that Lucrezia was still *virgo intacta*. This the Pope considered a good reason for divorce.

Sforza was furious at the implication of his impotence and begged the help of his cousin and ally, the Duke of Milan. But the Duke was afraid of a renewed French invasion, when the help of the Pope might be necessary to him; and he dared not offend the latter.

He suggested that the Pope should let Sforza prove the implication to be false by giving proof of his potency before a Papal Legate and a selected council. This had been practised in the past when it was necessary for a man to demonstrate his powers.

Sforza, humiliated and outraged, refused such a public display as beneath his dignity. The Duke then suggested that he might be tested with selected courtesans in the presence of the Legate. This again Sforza indignantly rejected. It was easy then for the Duke to placate the Pope by pretending to believe the story of Sforza's impotence.

The Pope accordingly went ahead with his plans for Lucrezia, and meanwhile sent his daughter to the Convent of St. Sixtus to await the result.

*   *   *

Cesare's jealousy of Juan had now grown to such proportions that he was determined to appease it, and he made his plans.

His opportunity came when Vannozza invited both her sons to visit her. Vannozza adored these two magnificent sons of hers for whom she believed a glorious future was in store; but Cesare remained the favourite of all her children and it must have been a great delight when he found time to visit her. This he probably did frequently, for she never failed to give him the adoration he demanded, and the terrible cruelty he meted out to those who had looted her house during the French invasion, indicates the regard he felt for her.

Vannozza had decided to give a supper party. It was June and hot; therefore she did not give the party in her Rome residence but in her vineyard which was between the churches of San Martino ai Monti and Santa Lucia in Selce.

There were other guests besides Vannozza's two sons but it was an intimate party. Cesare had discarded his Cardinal's robes and put on his rich layman's garb; but Juan outshone him with his jewels and gay manners.

How proud Vannozza must have been. Juan a great soldier and a Spanish Duke. Cesare a great Cardinal and destined to be the Holy Father himself. It was true that there were rumours in the City regarding these sons of hers. Cesare inspired fear wherever he went, but she dotingly believed that was a sign of his greatness. There would be many to envy her Cesare. There was Juan, more handsome perhaps than Cesare, but, in her fond eyes, more conventionally so; he was great, her Juan, but Cesare was the greatest man in Italy, and, she would be ready to swear, in the whole world. It was said that no beautiful young women—or young men—were safe once Juan had cast his eyes upon them, and that when Juan said 'Come hither!', to Juan they must go or suffer the consequences of insulting the Borgia dignity. To Vannozza this seemed exactly as it should be. The two most powerful men—under His Holiness—were her two sons.

Perhaps Cesare was thinking on similar lines and making up his mind that in the future there must be only one son of the Pope to make his presence felt in Rome.

When they took leave of their mother and stepfather and the few guests who had made up the company, a masked figure appeared in the vineyard and asked softly for the Duke of Gandia. Juan greeted this masked person with pleasure. All present believed it was his newest lover, the sex of whom was as yet unknown, for Juan had been seen in the streets of Rome in the last weeks accompanied by a masked person to whom he seemed devoted.

The brothers said their farewells to Vannozza and her husband, and left, the masked figure riding pillion with Juan.

Each brother was surrounded by his attendants, but when they reached the Ponte district, Juan announced that he was leaving the rest of them at that spot. He and his masked friend would ride off with one groom only in attendance. His attendants begged to be allowed to go with him; they said the hour was late and the district was not a safe one to be alone in at this hour. Juan shrugged them aside and of course none dared disobey.

Cesare with his attendants and those of his brother continued his journey to the Vatican.

It seemed clear to everyone that Juan had an engagement with his masked friend. This was evidently so, for when he reached the Piazza degli Ebrei, he instructed the groom to wait there for him and, if he did not return in an hour, to go home.

This was the last time Juan was seen alive. He was soon missed next day, and when Alexander heard the news he was filled with alarm. Search parties were sent out and, before very many hours had passed, Juan's groom was found in the deserted Piazza degli Ebrei, stabbed to death.

A Dalmatian boatman, who lived in his boat which was moored on the banks of the Tiber, then came forward and said that he had seen a man approach the river leading a white horse over which was slung something which might have been a body. A man on horseback had given instructions as to what was to be done and the boatman had heard him addressed as 'My Lord'. The body had been thrown into the river and the dead man's cloak floated, bearing him up for a while; then he who had been addressed as 'My Lord' ordered that stones be thrown at the cloak; this was done and soon the cloak and body were seen no more.

When asked why he did not immediately report what he had seen, the boatman shrugged his shoulders and declared that there was nothing very unusual in seeing a body cast into the Tiber.

The river was dragged and Juan's body recovered. There were ducats in his purse and no attempt had been made to wrench the jewels from his collar.

Alexander was in despair. Not only had he lost his best-loved son, but also many of his immediate hopes. Cesare, destined for the Church, could bring no legitimate offspring to the Borgias, and Joffré was young as yet.

The body of Juan was washed and perfumed and decked out in his ducal garments of splendour, and there was a procession which walked from St. Angelo to the Borgia Chapel in Santa Maria del Popolo through the night to the accompaniment of dirges, while Alexander sat at his window sobbing in grief so unrestrained that the people wondered what terrible revenge would be taken when the murderers of his son were discovered.

Afterwards Alexander shut himself away for several days, so great was his anguish, and during that time he suffered acutely from the fainting fits which were probably caused by high blood-pressure. He declared that if he had seven papacies he would give them all if in exchange his son could be returned to him alive and well.

Rumour was rife throughout Rome, and all were waiting for the arrest of the murderers. Many were suspected, chiefly Sforza. It was said that he had done the deed out of jealousy for his wife, Lucrezia, who had been the mistress of her brother Juan.

The identity of the masked person was never discovered; but quite suddenly the Pope ordered that there should be no more investigations into the murder; and this gave rise to the belief, which has persisted, that he was aware of the identity of the man who had organized the murder: Cesare.

* * *

Alexander's attitude towards Cesare changed at this time. Strangely enough, instead of hating him for the murder of Juan, he lavished on him all the love that had been Juan's. His great desire seemed to be to heap honours on Cesare, to make him combine the wealth and standing of his brother with his own.

At the same time, there were some who noticed that Alexander seemed a little afraid of Cesare, as though he were wondering what kind of son he had produced, and what dark thoughts went on behind those smouldering cynical eyes. It seemed at times that he placated Cesare and that he tried to woo him with tenderness as well as with promises of great favours.

Cesare took advantage of the change in his father's attitude to demand that he be released from the Church and that Joffré should take his place. He wanted a divorce arranged between Joffré and Sanchia, and since Sanchia's family should not be insulted, and since if he married her he might become one of the heirs to the throne of Naples, he would make her his wife when she was no longer Joffré's.

Alexander was astounded, but it is clear that he had come to believe that when Cesare made up his mind that he wanted something he would not rest until it was his.

The Pope's nature was a happy one and he was incapable of entertaining grief for any length of time. A few weeks after his public demonstration of anguish over Juan's death, he seemed suddenly to forget he had ever had a son of that name. All his tenderness, all his schemes were now concentrated on Cesare and Lucrezia.

He longed to please Cesare by bringing about his release from the Church, but when he considered what trouble had been caused when he had had to make him legitimate in order to give him a Cardinal's hat, he realized that he would have to move very warily in this matter, for a great scandal would be created if he allowed Cesare to give up his Cardinalship and lead a secular life.

There was Lucrezia, still not divorced, and that was a matter which needed more immediate attention. Cesare agreed with the Pope in this, and for the time was content to turn his energies to freeing his sister from Sforza.

They had decided that Lucrezia's divorce should be obtained because of the inability of her husband to consummate the marriage. Lucrezia would have to leave her convent and come to the Vatican, where, before the Envoys and the Cardinals, she must swear that she was still *virgo intacta*, and it was for this reason only that she asked to be released from her marriage.

An awkward complication arose at this juncture. When Lucrezia was ready to come to the Vatican it was discovered that she was six months pregnant. It was going to prove rather a difficult ordeal for this girl with the innocent face to stand before these men of the Church and swear to her virginity when she was in such a condition. Of course, her dressmakers would do what was possible, and Lucrezia would be dressed in billowing skirts, but even so, at six months after conception, a pregnant woman was going to find it difficult to hide her state.

The Pope was alarmed, for it was more than six months before that Lucrezia had parted from her husband, and in any case he must be proclaimed impotent.

It would have been impossible to keep Lucrezia's condition secret from some, and her servants and attendants must be aware of it. This meant that after the divorce there would be scandal concerning Lucrezia, and the Pope was anxious to avoid this.

There was something else. The affair could be even more sinister. Six months previously, Cesare had visited his sister in her convent, and it was well known that they were on passionately loving terms. What a scandal if Lucrezia, declared *virgo intacta*, was not only pregnant, but pregnant with her own brother's child!

*   *   *

Meanwhile Lucrezia was summoned to the Vatican and before the judges conducted herself with such charm and seeming innocence that they were completely convinced that she spoke the truth when she declared that her marriage had not been consummated and she was still a virgin. Her devoted maid, Pantisilea, who of course was in the secret, had been so clever with her mistress's clothes, that the fact that she was soon to become a mother was completely concealed, and the divorce was granted.

But there was concern in the intimate apartments of the Pope. Several people were aware of Lucrezia's condition, and when the child was born, more would be. Something had to be done and done quickly.

There was among the Papal Chamberlains a young Spaniard named Pedro Caldes who was familiarly called Il Perotto. He was extremely handsome and charming, and the Pope had made use of him to send messages from the Vatican to the Convent when Lucrezia's divorce was being discussed. Il Perotto had called attention to himself by the devotion he had always shown towards Lucrezia, and all those about her had known that he was desperately in love with her; and now there was to be a child.

It is not known whether Lucrezia's condition was due to Pedro Caldes or her brother, and this has naturally been the cause of much controversy.

The Pope and Cesare professed to be deeply shocked when they discovered Lucrezia's condition, but they would make this pretence even if they had known of it from its early stages. They had to acknowledge the fact, that she was pregnant, among those who were aware of this; but they certainly could not let it be known, or suspected, that Cesare might be the father. Therefore naturally they would seek for a victim, and there was Pedro Caldes ready at hand.

They would have decided they must make him the scapegoat—whether he was guilty or whether they wanted him to take the blame in order to divert suspicion from Cesare. So one day when Cesare met Pedro near the Pope's apartment, he drew his sword and prepared to attack. Pedro, terrified, took to his heels and Cesare chased him right to the steps of the pontifical throne where the young Spaniard begged the Pope to save him. Alexander was prepared to do this, but Cesare thrust at him with his sword, and, we are told by the Venetian Ambassador who was present, the blood spurted up into the Pope's face.

It is not known whether or not Pedro escaped at that time, but shortly afterwards his body was discovered, bound hand and foot, in the River Tiber, and all knew that he had been despatched for having made Madonna Lucrezia pregnant.

It is sad that the little maid, Pantisilea, who had done nothing but help her mistress in her difficulty should also have been murdered. Her body was recovered from the river on the same day as was that of Pedro Caldes. Pantisilea had been, it was said, the mistress of the Pope at one time; this makes the deed even more horrible; and it seems that Alexander, at this time, was falling more and more under the influence of Cesare, who was utterly ruthless.

Lucrezia gave birth to a son and there is still a certain amount of controversy concerning this child. Some, of course, believe that he was the son of Pedro Caldes; but there is strong support for the theory that the child was Cesare's for, three years after his birth, a child was brought to the Vatican. He was known as the *Infante Romano* and was deeply loved by Alexander. He was given the name of Giovanni Borgia and had his place at all functions, and was eventually accepted as one of the heirs to the Borgia fortune. Alexander endowed him with great possessions, and this seems strange, as Cesare had other bastards, some of whom were ignored, and those who were acknowledged were never treated as was this little boy.

It would seem that the *Infante Romano* was deeply loved, especially by Alexander, because he was doubly Borgia, through his father and his mother.

There was yet another theory. The Pope loved his daughter as tenderly and as passionately as her brother did. There had been rumours concerning Lucrezia and her father as insistent as there had been concerning Lucrezia and her brother. There are some who believe that the *Infante Romano* was not the son of Cesare but was nevertheless a Borgia, and that the Pope's fond affection meant that the *Infante* was the son of none other than Alexander himself.

*   *   *

It was immediately necessary to find another husband for
Lucrezia, and a marriage was arranged for her with the young
brother of Sanchia of Aragon, Alfonso, the young Duke of
Bisceglie and Prince of Quadrata. He was seventeen, Lucrezia
eighteen; and this young man was handsome and amazingly
like his sister Sanchia.

Lucrezia was so delighted with him when he made his
appearance in Rome that, during the ceremonies, the Pope
remarked that the young people seemed anxious to be done
with the formalities and get on with the love-making.

This was true. For the first time Lucrezia had a lover who
could make her forget her brother; and although the young
bridegroom had been reluctant to come to Rome—being
terrified of what he would find waiting for him when he got
there, imagining no doubt a lewd and alarming woman—
when he saw his bride with the lovely innocent looks, so ready
to love him, he was enchanted.

Sforza had protested fiercely against the divorce of himself
and Lucrezia, and had declared that the accusation of impotence had been set in motion by the Pope because he wished to
have Lucrezia for his own mistress. It may have been this
remark which gave rise to the scandal concerning the *Infante
Romano's* being the Pope's own son, for it was during the
divorce proceedings that the private life of the Borgias was
exposed in all its horror to the marvelling citizens of Rome.
It was then that the incest which prevailed in the Pope's
family was discussed throughout Italy and the world; and the
way in which the enemies of the family had fatal accidents or
suffered sudden or lingering deaths was also discussed.

The very name of Borgia made many shudder, and those who
came into contact with any member of the Pope's family were
learning to be very wary.

It was said they experimented with poisons and improved
on those methods which were known to them through the
Spanish Moors. Their drugs improved the flavour of food and
wine. No one but the Borgias knew the ingredients of their
poisons. The name *cantarella* was whispered with dread; this
was the famous Borgia poison, which appears to have been some
form of white powder presumably containing arsenic, for the
basis of many poisons of the era was arsenic. It resembled sugar
and the refining methods of the Borgias had rendered it almost
tasteless. Another poison which was used by the Borgias was the
famous *aqua toffana* which again was some solution of arsenic,
also rendered tasteless. It appears that this could be moderated
to produce immediate death or a long and lingering illness.

Aquetta di Napoli was another of their concoctions; colourless, without smell or taste, it was ideal for their purposes. This was reputed to bring about a wasting disease, which produced anxiety and great fear in its first stages, followed by constant and agonizing pain. The time of death, it was said, was decided by the poisoners.

Thus it was a very pleasant surprise for the young Duke to find, instead of a monster, a charming young girl, only a little older than himself, ready to be his very loving wife. There was His Holiness joining in the revels, almost like a boy himself, making jokes and playing pranks, enjoying the somewhat lewd insinuations concerning the bridal pair which might have been expected in some company but surely not in that of the Vicar of Christ.

Cesare may have terrified him. Cesare was never happy to see Lucrezia in love with a husband, for that seemed to him the height of infidelity.

But the fears of young Alfonso would temporarily have been soothed, for he had nothing to fear from Cesare at this time since Cesare was too deeply concerned with his own affairs.

*   *   *

Since Lucrezia had married Sanchia's brother, there was no need for a marriage between Cesare and Sanchia, for the alliance with Naples was now cemented.

Cesare's great plan was therefore to break away from the Church and show his prowess in the military field. Alexander continued to despair of freeing Cesare from the Church, for he realized that there was a limit beyond which even he might not go; but he disliked disappointing his son, and indeed seemed to be afraid of disappointing him.

Then it seemed suddenly as though the way was made clear to him.

Charles VIII had died and Louis XII had mounted the throne of France. Louis was not satisfied with his marriage and wanted to divorce his wife that he might be free to marry Anne of Brittany, who was the widow of the deceased Charles. A divorce was impossible without the permission of the Pope. It was because of this that Alexander saw a way of satisfying Cesare.

If he supported Louis in his desires, then he could ask Louis to support him in his. In fact he would make it clear that if Louis refused his help regarding Cesare, there would be no divorce.

Ambitious French eyes were turned on Italy, and there was

consideration of pressing claims to the Kingdom of Naples which, the French asserted, belonged in reality to the House of Anjou in spite of the fact that it was now occupied by the usurping House of Aragon. They declared that Milan, through the House of Orléans, belonged also to the French; and now that they were strong, they saw no reason why they should not set out to claim what was theirs by right.

In view of the consternation this state of affairs would cause in Naples and Milan, the support of Louis would be well worth having in the Vatican and would give the Holy Father bargaining powers with the recalcitrant Cardinals who represented the Duchy of Milan and the Kingdom of Naples.

He was ready therefore to make a pact with the King of France, and conveyed the news to him that he would put no obstacles in the way of Louis' divorce—at a price.

Alexander was a master in the art of diplomacy, and the price he now demanded was support to free Cesare from the Church, a French Dukedom for Cesare when he was free, and a Princess to be Cesare's wife.

Louis wanted his divorce so badly that he was ready to agree to this.

Louis had his divorce; and the Pope declared—with French support—that to keep Cesare in the Church against his will would be to imperil his immortal soul. So Cesare became Duke of Valence—he was known as Duc de Valentinois in France and as Il Valentino or Valenza in Italy, which was partly due to the fact that he had been the Archbishop of Valencia—which Dukedom carried with it a revenue of ten thousand scudi a year; and he was to go to France that Louis might find a bride for him.

Cynical Cardinals watching these manœuvres said: "Beware of the designs of the Father and the Son, for the Holy Ghost has little to say in the matter."

*   *   *

So Cesare went to France, his evil reputation travelling before him. Moreover it showed itself upon his face, for he had been suffering for some time from syphilis—the *mal francese*—and it had left unpleasant stigmata on his face, which at close quarters completely destroyed that beauty which had been his.

He travelled ostentatiously, and the cost of the journey was paid for by taxes levied on the Jews, who dared not complain, for the Spanish Inquisition had been set up in Italy.

The display was not received well in France for Louis was notoriously parsimonious, and the French gave out sly hints that they had expected a bastard—even a Pope's bastard—to travel more humbly.

Cesare's pride had not diminished with the years, nor had his bad temper; he watched those of his attendants who appeared to have noticed French slights, and made a mental note that when they returned to Rome they should be given a little dose of something to prevent their spreading tales. He knew now that his future was in the balance. He planned to make a brilliant marriage, to secure for himself the crown of Naples, and eventually unite all Italy under his rule. His first task was to persuade Louis to arrange a marriage for him with Sanchia's cousin, the legitimately born Carlotta of Naples. Carlotta was King Federico's daughter; her mother had been French and she was being educated at the Court of France.

He had set his ambitions too high, however, for there was consternation and indignation throughout the Courts of Europe at the prospect of a bastard Borgia marrying a royal, legitimate Princess; and Louis, who was indignant at the high price the Pope had demanded for his divorce, was pleased in his shrewd sly way at the discomfiture of the Pope's arrogant son.

The longer Cesare dallied in France, the more insolent those tales became which were spread about him in that country; they were even repeated in Rome. Alexander was growing anxious about the friendship with France. To make matters more intolerable, Carlotta was married to a Breton Baron.

Cesare had no help for it but to continue in France waiting for Louis to provide him with a wife.

He was at last given sixteen-year-old Charlotte d'Albret, daughter of the King of Navarre; they were married at Blois, and Cesare continued to stay in France.

*   *   *

Lucrezia meanwhile was enjoying a happy married life with young Alfonso. To Alfonso's great delight she was pregnant, and he eagerly awaited the birth of the child.

Unfortunately two months after its conception Lucrezia and some of her girl attendants were visiting a neighbouring vineyard, and in a sudden rush of high spirits Lucrezia suggested a race. Lucrezia's slipper caught in the flounces of her gown and she stumbled to the ground, while one of the girls who was immediately behind her fell on her. She fainted and had to be carried back to the Palace. That day she had a miscarriage.

There was mourning throughout the Vatican, and the Pope

seemed almost as grieved as he had been by the loss of Juan; but very soon afterwards, when a carnival was held in Rome, he and Lucrezia were seen together on the balcony at the Castel Saint Angelo laughing heartily at the masques and processions which were, in accordance with custom, decidedly bawdy; and the more lewd the images and pictures and gestures of the performers, the more delight—so those who saw them pointed out—did the Pope and his daughter express.

Perhaps Lucrezia missed Cesare less than she would have believed possible. She was ready to be quite devoted to her young husband, as he was to her. Lucrezia, it seemed, in her early years took her character from her surroundings; she was ready to be all that was demanded of her, and it was her misfortune that she was born into a family of vicious sensualists. But Lucrezia was beginning to understand something of politics and she knew that, as Cesare had failed to secure Carlotta as a bride, and with her the crown of Naples, he would not rest until that crown was his; and she foresaw strife ahead.

Cesare had written to his father, giving an account of his wedding night; and knowing that the Pope would be interested in the most intimate details, he had not omitted these, but had indeed stressed them. The letter caused Alexander much amusement and he boasted to the Cardinals and officials that the King of France had congratulated Cesare on the prowess he showed in the marriage bed.

The Cardinals were less inclined to share in the fun, for they knew that Louis was not the man to give something for nothing, and that he had his eyes on Naples and Milan and would expect the Vatican to be his ally when he set out on their conquest.

Lucrezia, however, allowed herself to forget these politics, for she was pregnant once more, and this time was determined to let no accident interfere with the bearing of a child.

*   *   *

The Cardinals had been right in their fear. The French crossed the Alps and prepared to take Milan. Ludovico, the Duke of Milan, tried to raise help. Maximilian of Austria was himself at war with the Swiss and had no help to offer; and finding himself without allies, Ludovico fled to Austria. Milan was now open to French conquest, other Italian states standing aside, hoping that Louis would be content with Milan.

Much to the chagrin of the Cardinals, Alexander invited Louis to Rome for the Christmas Mass in St. Peter's; Alexander

merely laughed when he was reminded that a short time before
he had fled before the armies of a King of France. He was now
allied with the French through the marriage of Cesare, and he
hoped for much from his new allies. At the same time he was
enough of a diplomatist to show friendship for the Houses of
Aragon and Naples, and those who were cautiously watching
his actions were uncertain whose friend he was.

But Lucrezia's husband, realizing that when Cesare returned
to Rome he, Alfonso, would be in acute danger, decided that
his best plan would be to emulate his predecessor, so he fled
from Rome one night without telling anyone that he was going.
Lucrezia, who was very near her confinement, was heart-
broken at the loss of her husband.

From Naples, Alfonso wrote to Lucrezia, begging her to
join him there, but the letter was intercepted by Alexander
who could not bear the thought of losing his daughter, and,
fearing that she might attempt to go to her husband, he placed
her under guard. Afraid that Alfonso's sister Sanchia would do
all in her power to persuade Lucrezia to join her husband, he
banished his daughter-in-law from the Vatican.

Eventually he realized that if he kept Lucrezia a prisoner
she might attempt to escape, and hating to be on bad terms
with his beloved daughter, he made her Regent of Spoleto, a
city which before this had never been governed by any but
men of high rank such as Cardinals. With a letter which
Alexander had written to the Priors of Spoleto, telling them that
the Holy Office expected them to accept her as their Regent
and submit to her in all things, Lucrezia set out.

When she arrived at Spoleto, Alexander ordered Alfonso to
join her there, which eventually he did.

Lucrezia did not stay long in Spoleto—merely long enough
that all might know that the Pope had bestowed this rich
territory on his daughter. He also intended to grant her the
baronial fief of Nepi; to Nepi Lucrezia went with Alfonso and
there the Pope was waiting to greet them.

Cesare joined them at Nepi. If he was angered by the
sight of Lucrezia and her husband, he would have given no
sign; but it may have been that his head was too full of his own
affairs. It was at Nepi that he and the Pope discussed the
grandiose plans for the future.

With the help of the French, to whom he was now allied
through marriage, Cesare planned first to dominate Romagna
and then the whole of Italy. Cesare saw himself at that time as
the future ruler of Italy and perhaps the world.

A few weeks later Lucrezia with her husband and father

returned to Rome and, on the 1st of November, 1499, Lucrezia's
son, Roderigo, was born.

*   *   *

The Pope was enraptured by his grandchild, and the baptism
was an occasion of splendour. Lucrezia received the homage
and congratulations of all the most important people in Rome
lying in her bed decorated with gold and red satin, while the
room in which she lay had been especially hung with velvet
of the new blue colour which was called Alexandrine.

To the baptismal ceremony, which was conducted in the
Sistine Chapel, preceded by chamberlains and Papal guards
and dressed in rose-coloured cloth, came Juan Cervillon, the
famous Spanish soldier who had been given the honour of
carrying the baby. At the altar he handed the child to the
Archbishop of Cosenza who carried it to the silver font.

To the almost childish pleasure of the Pope, the little boy
was named after him: Roderigo.

It was a week after this event when Cesare arrived in Rome.
He came incognito and he had many scores to settle. He could
not have been very pleased to see Lucrezia happy in her
marriage, nor could he have been so delighted with the new
baby as his father was. Many incidents lived on in his memory.
Cesare's pride had increased with the years. He had suffered
great humiliation in France, where he had not found it so easy
to register his displeasure as in his own country. Students of the
University of Paris had acted comedies based on his life and his
marriage. The Pope and Lucrezia had not figured very favour-
ably in these burlesques. Moreover, the French had a pungent
wit which could be wounding. Louis had pretended to be
annoyed by his subjects, but Cesare had a notion that he had
enjoyed his friend's discomfiture as much as anyone.

With Cesare's return it began to be realized throughout
Italy what happened to those who offended the Borgias. The
outbreak of sudden death was like an epidemic which swept the
country.

The Borgia terror had begun in earnest.

Alexander was approaching seventy, and he seemed to come
at this time under the domination of Cesare. Cesare set the
pace. He was completely ruthless. The lives of his enemies
seemed without worth to him. He removed them as he would
irritating flies.

It was noticed that many of those who had accompanied
him to France disappeared. Some were found in the Tiber,
some stabbed to death in the narrow alleys of Rome; but most

died mysteriously through the now famous Borgia dose. People shuddered as they talked of *cantarella*, *aqua toffana* and *aquetta di Napoli*.

Cesare was now reputed to employ Italian sorcerers to perfect the old recipes of the Spanish Moors.

Any who lived near the Borgias must be in danger of losing their lives; it might be that they, unwittingly, were privy to certain matters which the Borgias decided should be kept secret. It mattered not if these people were prepared to keep Borgia secrets; the Borgias took no chances. Spotted hemlock, monkshood and yew, henbane and the juice of the poppy, all formed the ingredients of those potions which the Borgias and their servants prepared so frequently for those guests from whom they might have something to fear, or on whom they wished to avenge themselves.

The slightest incident might put a person on the death list. A young constable of the guards who had been a favourite of Cesare's was found in the Tiber. There could have been no reason for his death except that he may have witnessed some humiliation of Cesare by the French.

Juan Cervillon, who had been honoured by being allowed to hold Lucrezia's little Roderigo at the baptism, asked for permission to leave Rome for Naples where his family lived. Permission was given; but Cervillon was never allowed to reach Naples. He knew too many Papal secrets. He was stabbed to death after leaving a supper party.

Yet when there was an attempt to poison the Pope, the Borgias were full of outraged anger. Poison was *their* prerogative; it seemed insolent, arrogant and callous to turn their own weapons against themselves. To Cesare this did not seem a natural outcome, as it would to normal people. Cesare saw himself as a god, looming above his fellows, a privileged person to deal death as he thought fit; that there should have been some form of retaliation astounded and infuriated him.

Suspicion of plotting against the Pope's life fell on Caterina Sforza, who was the illegitimate daughter of Duke Galeazzo Maria Sforza; and the enraged Cesare set out on a punitive expedition. In any case Caterina's two cities of Imola and Forli were on the list of those which Cesare had intended to capture.

Caterina was a woman of power. She had married at sixteen the Count of Forli who had been noted even in those days for his brutality. He had married Caterina for the dowry she brought him, but Caterina was quite capable of looking after herself. She had been inured to violence from the time she had seen her father done to brutal death outside the Cathedral of Milan; shortly after her marriage she had seen her husband brutally murdered by a mob which attacked their castle, and his naked body flung from the battlements. She married again, and her second husband was murdered in a similar manner. Caterina, by this time a woman of strong determination, lusty and bloodthirsty as either of her husbands, sent an avenging party to those villages where her husband's assassins lived, and had every woman, man and child therein brutally murdered. She then ruled her domain with the help of her numerous lovers whom she used and discarded at will.

It was this woman whom Cesare set out to subdue. Caterina's subjects, ready enough to escape from her harsh rule, surrendered Imola without a fight, but Caterina, who was in the castle of Forli, fortified herself there, and put up a fierce resistance.

Cesare was determined on victory, determined to capture the whole of Romagna and make himself lord of that dominion. Caterina was eventually forced to capitulate. On entering the castle he demanded the *droit de seigneur* and sent a detailed account to his father of his adventure with Caterina. Not that Caterina would be loth to surrender to the *droit*. She had had many lovers and was as lustful as Cesare, and it is probable that the very fact that he was an enemy, of evil reputation, added to her debased pleasure.

She was installed as a prisoner in the Belvedere, that lovely villa surrounded by pine and orange trees, and there was treated well. Later she was taken to the fortress of Castel Saint Angelo.

Cesare had begun his conquest of Romagna.

*   *   *

The Pope was in his seventies, and even a man of his abounding vitality could not be expected to live much longer. Cesare was afraid that his father would die before he, Cesare, had achieved his ambition, and was wise enough to know that if this should happen his position would be a dangerous one.

Throughout Italy all spoke with caution of Il Valentino or Valenza. The Borgia terror was increasing. Tongues were cut out if an ill word was spoken against a Borgia by the humblest fisherman or woodcutter in a cheap tavern; and a look was enough to constitute an insult.

Those who were in Cesare's service were in the greatest danger of all. Men made their wills and their peace with God before they supped with the Borgias.

In Cesare's camp in Romagna the Portuguese Bishop of Ceuta, Ferdinando d'Almaida died suddenly. He had done good service for Cesare when in France; but he must have ceased to be useful.

No one knew to whom the Borgia 'powder' would be given next.

* * *

One day lightning struck the Vatican and the ceiling in the Pope's apartment was dislodged. He was seated under the canopy on his throne, and with him were the Bishop of Capua and a chamberlain. A cloud of dust filled the room and the masonry was seen to fall on the throne. It seemed impossible that he could have survived.

"The Pope is dead!" cried all in the Vatican; and the news was carried through the streets.

It was discovered that a thunderbolt had hit the Vatican and passed through three floors to that room in which the Pope was sitting. It took a long time to dig him out from the rubble but, when this was done, it was found that the Pope was by no means dead. He was, it was true, suffering from one of his fainting fits, but he soon recovered from that.

The vitality of this old man was truly amazing, and it was said that the Borgias had some supernatural power, and as they were evil that power must come from the devil. Cesare had, immediately before the Vatican was hit, left a chamber in which three guards were killed by the collapse of the ceiling.

The Pope appeared to be immortal; and it was clear that he wished his son Cesare to be the ruler of all Italy.

* * *

Cesare's triumphs came to a temporary halt when the Emperor Maximilian gave that aid to Ludovico which enabled him to recapture Milan. The French were obliged to withdraw certain of the troops which they had lent to Cesare, which meant that he found himself unable to continue with his conquests. There was nothing for him to do but return to Rome that he might attempt to raise funds and a new army.

He made a triumphal entry into Rome; but as a member of the family, Cardinal Juan Borgia, had recently died (he had expired mysteriously after having left Cesare's camp, and it was suspected that a little dose of Borgia 'powder' may have been responsible), Cesare decided that, to show his grief at the death of his relative, the entry, although he was a victorious general returning from the wars, should tell the whole of Rome that the family was in mourning.

Cesare himself was dressed in plain black velvet—but it was the most expensive velvet and perfectly made. The carriages were covered with black materials, and the Swiss guards were in black velvet and wore dark plumes. The troops marched soundlessly through the City until they arrived at Castel Saint Angelo; then the fireworks were let off.

It was all very impressive, but the rumours that the Cardinal was yet another Borgia victim persisted.

Now that he was in Rome Cesare looked with distaste on the happiness of his sister and young Alfonso of Bisceglie.

Alfonso, while terrified of his brother-in-law, continued deeply enamoured of his wife. He let himself believe that if Cesare wanted to harm him, Lucrezia would never allow that to happen. He knew that there were three people for whom Cesare had some regard—his father, his mother and his sister. Cesare could see no virtue in people who were not related to him; and even they were only worthy of his regard because he felt they were in some measure part of himself.

It was July—a beautiful summer's night—and Alfonso had been visiting Lucrezia and Sanchia, his sister. He had had supper with the Pope, and with two of his attendants he left the Vatican by the door under the loggia of Benediction. Chatting pleasantly with his men, as he went towards the palace of Santa Maria in Portico, he noticed a group of people sprawling on the steps of St. Peter's. He thought they might be pilgrims or perhaps beggars, and as they called to him he went towards them to give them alms.

The men immediately sprang into action and Alfonso and his two attendants were surrounded. From their muffling garments these men produced daggers; one held Alfonso by the throat, and another had him pinioned.

Alfonso was young and strong; he, with his men, struggled and called for help, and their cries brought out the Papal guards. As the guards approached, the 'pilgrims', evidently feeling they would be unwise to linger whether they had accomplished their mission or not, ran off in the direction of the Tiber.

Alfonso was carried into the Vatican to the apartments of Lucrezia and Sanchia, who, both loving him dearly, were horrified by what they saw. Some of his attendants gave a breathless and hysterical account of what had happened, and as he lay fainting at his wife's feet, Alfonso murmured that he knew this to be the work of Cesare.

Lucrezia must have been horrified at Cesare's wanton attempt to destroy her happiness. What could her feelings have been at that moment towards her brother? There must have been fear and hatred, yet, in view of events, it seems certain that Cesare was then, and as long as he lived, the most important person in Lucrezia's life. They were bound together by that inescapable and indestructible closeness which can only be called love.

Yet now Lucrezia sought to protect her husband from her brother. The only way of explaining her emotions at this time seems to be that her love for her husband was a purely physical emotion; he was young and handsome; she also was young; both needed constant physical satisfaction which the other supplied; it would be a new and satisfying experience to Lucrezia when this could be obtained legitimately, and she was eager to keep her young husband alive and with her. But for Cesare she felt that dark and brooding passion, that bond which held them close together and which neither of them could—even if they would—sever. In time Lucrezia would have grown tired of her husband and taken other lovers; then he would have ceased to be of great importance to her. But no matter what tragedy Cesare brought into her life, as later events proved, she was always ready to be his slave.

Now Lucrezia begged her father to give his protection to her husband, and this Alexander promised to do. True to his word he gave Alfonso a room in the Vatican close to his own apartments; this room was well guarded, and the ambassador from Naples was called in to watch the dressing of Alfonso's wounds so that, explained the Pope, none should say that poison had been introduced into his body at an opportune moment.

At first it seemed as though Alfonso was mortally wounded, but under the care of Lucrezia and Sanchia he began to improve.

Both Lucrezia and Sanchia were determined that he should get well. To Sanchia he was her handsome young brother, and Sanchia had a score to settle with Cesare who had once talked of marrying her and then had declined to do so in favour of Carlotta of Naples, Sanchia's cousin who possessed the added attraction of legitimate birth. As he had eventually married Charlotte d'Albret, Sanchia considered herself doubly slighted. Her passion for Cesare had never been anything like tender love; and now that she knew him for the would-be murderer of her young brother, she would have been determined—apart from her desire to avenge herself—to flout Cesare.

As for Lucrezia, she was longing for the return to health of her husband.

So, since the air was always full of poison rumours, these two women decided that they alone would cook Alfonso's meals and they alone would look after him. Thus they would make sure that the usual method of removing an enemy was not employed.

Alfonso's mother came to see him and brought with her physicians from the King of Naples; and surrounded by these, and the two women whom he trusted, the will to recover came to him so strongly that, in spite of the terrible wounds he had received, there was hope that he would live.

Rumour filled the streets. Who had attempted to kill Alfonso? Why was the assassin not brought to book? The Pope might apologize to the Neapolitan Ambassador, but what did he do about bringing the scoundrels to justice? Nothing. And the reason? It was because the Pope knew that the guiding hand in this affair was the same as that which had brought about the murder of the Pope's own son Juan: Cesare Borgia.

Cesare was furious because his assassins had failed. Passionately he desired the death of Alfonso, not only because he could not endure the thought of his happiness with Lucrezia, but because, if Alfonso died, the House of Aragon would never forgive Alexander, and the Pope would therefore be forced to strengthen his alliance with the French. Cesare pinned much of his hopes on the help he would receive from the French King to enable him to subdue all Italy.

*   *   *

Alfonso was able to walk about his room and take a little exercise in the Pope's private garden. He was well on the way to recovery.

But Cesare had made up his mind that he should not recover.

One warm August day Sanchia and Lucrezia left the sick room for an hour or so; they had one or two missions in the town, and as Alfonso was so much better they chose that day on which to fulfil them. This is the account of the Florentine Ambassador which does not agree in every detail with other contemporary recorders, but it is plausible, and in any case the differences have no effect on the essential features of the story.

Cesare chose this time to send his men to Alfonso's room and arrest everyone therein on a charge of plotting against the Borgias.

Lucrezia and Sanchia, being warned that this was happening, hurried back to Alfonso and, seeing the men there, demanded an explanation. Don Micheletto Corella, on being questioned by Lucrezia, told her that he was acting on orders; he suggested that if she wished to countermand those orders she could do so on the authority of the Pope. Lucrezia and

Sanchia rushed to the Pope's apartment. He was not to be found. Some authorities believe that he was now working with Cesare and that he had deliberately absented himself, being warned of what was to take place.

Unable to find him, Lucrezia and Sanchia hurried back to Alfonso. There was no one there but Alfonso. His body was lying across the bed, and they saw that he had been strangled.

*   *   *

Cesare made no attempt to deny that he was the instigator of that particular murder. He declared that Alfonso had sought to take his life, and that when he, Cesare, had been walking in the Pope's garden, Alfonso had shot his crossbow at him.

Here was another scandal to undermine the sanctity of the Vatican, and Alexander was disturbed. But as was his habit, when anything unpleasant happened, he wished to forget it as quickly as possible. The easiest course open to him was to accept Cesare's explanation, and to say that if Alfonso had been murdered by Cesare, he deserved his fate as he had tried to murder Cesare.

But to satisfy the Neapolitans, Alexander had to promise that there should be an enquiry into the case. This he conveniently forgot and within a few weeks he was acting as though the murder of a Prince of Naples had never taken place.

As for Cesare, he was given as much respect as ever. The Cardinals dreaded yet revered him; he was received with acclaim in the Church, and prelates regarded it an honour to receive the red hat through him; Cesare cynically sold this honour to those who could pay most highly for it.

Although he did not care who should know that he was a murderer, when he went into the streets of Rome, he invariably wore a mask. This was not only in fear of retaliation, but to cover up the hideous disfigurements which were becoming more pronounced on his once beautiful face. There had been several bouts of the *mal francese* and, although there were temporary cures, each left its mark upon him.

*   *   *

His daughter's grief at the loss of her husband irritated Alexander, who could not bear to contemplate sorrow. He wanted gaiety all about him, so he sent Lucrezia away from Rome to stay at the castle of Nepi until she should forget her grief and again be the gay daughter whom the Pope so loved to have with him. Sanchia, who also grieved for her brother, was banished; but the two were not allowed to be together.

Always eager to consolidate his position during the lifetime of the Pope, Cesare prepared to set out for military conquest.

On his journey he visited his sister, and this visit throws some light on the extraordinary relationship between brother and sister, for although Lucrezia is reported to have been bowed down with sorrow, and Cesare's visit took place only six weeks after the murder of Alfonso, this strange woman welcomed with joy her husband's murderer.

It is said that when she saw the banners of Cesare's soldiers at her gates, and when she came face to face with her brother, the *condottiere* in the midst of his captains, she seemed to throw off her listlessness and take on new life.

There is no record that Cesare was lover as well as brother during that brief visit, but it seems very likely that this was so, for how could one of Cesare's character, determined to dominate, and one of Lucrezia's, desirous of being dominated, have resisted this confirmation of that indestructible bond between them.

A few weeks after Cesare's visit, Lucrezia returned to Rome where her father eagerly awaited her and was ready to discuss her third marriage.

*   *   *

A marriage was arranged between Lucrezia and Alfonso d'Este, who was the eldest son of the Duke of Ferrara. Ferrara demanded a magnificent dowry on account of the Pope's bastard daughter, and even so it was clear that he was not eager to receive one of Lucrezia's reputation into his family.

Alexander was ready to pay the dowry. He knew that even his unbounded vitality could not keep him alive for ever, and that strong family feeling was as evident as it ever was. He wanted to see his children secure before he died.

Cesare had secured great military triumphs; he was now the Duke of Romagna and appeared to be all-powerful; but the Pope was uneasy, knowing his son to be surrounded by enemies who, although eager to retain his friendship now, at the least sign of disaster would turn against him.

There were times when Alexander was alarmed—or would have been if he had allowed himself to brood on this—by Cesare's violent rages. It seemed that Cesare's periodic bouts of the *mal francese* were affecting his mind. If he were crossed he gave expression to his anger in a brutality which was growing more and more sadistic and savage.

There had been such brutality at the massacre of Capua that it would never be forgotten in Italian history. Forty virgins

had been captured in Naples and sent to Rome to administer
to the pleasure of Cesare when his military campaigns permitted.
He was regarded with horror by all with whom he came into
contact, and Alexander wondered where this would end.

Cesare was as eager as the Pope for the marriage of Lucrezia
and Alfonso d'Este, because of the political advantages it
offered; but he was as angry as ever at the thought of another's
possessing Lucrezia.

There were many who said that before Lucrezia left for
Ferrara, Cesare took great delight in debauching her, and that
Lucrezia was nothing loth to spend her nights with the mur-
derer of the husband whom she had professed to love so dearly.

There is no proof of this, but there is proof that those orgies,
organized by Cesare for the enjoyment of his family, really did
take place.

Perhaps the most notorious of these is the ballet of the
chestnuts, when Cesare brought fifty courtesans into his
apartment at the Vatican. The duty of these courtesans was
to dance with Cesare's servants and other gentlemen gathered
in Cesare's apartment for the purpose. First the courtesans
danced in their clothes and then without them; and when the
dancing was over, hot roasted chestnuts were thrown on to the
floor, and the naked courtesans then scrambled for these, holding lighted candles in their hands as they did so. Lucrezia
afterwards presented prizes of silken gowns, shoes, berets and
other fine garments to those who, in the opinion of the judges,
had pandered most successfully to the low taste of the spectators
in their behaviour with the courtesans.

On another occasion two woodcutters were passing the
Vatican with their carts drawn by mares when they were
stopped by the Papal servants who took their mares from them
and led them into a courtyard of the Palace. From a balcony
Lucrezia and the Pope looked on while four stallions were let
loose in the courtyard. This is an indication of how bestial
behaviour had become under Alexander, for both he and his
daughter, it is reported from several sources, watched, with the
utmost delight, the fight of the four stallions for the two mares.

Obscene plays and masques, which had always amused the
Pope, were performed regularly in those days preceding
Lucrezia's departure for Ferrara.

And at length the wedding procession left Rome.

*   *   *

In the next year Cesare enjoyed many military triumphs, and
with each passing week his reputation grew more evil. There is

no doubt that he was guilty of mass murder, but it must be remembered that it had become the custom to lay the death of every prominent person at his door. He was fond of the fine arts and took the best artists into his service. It was in the year 1502 that Leonardo da Vinci became his fortress engineer. But throughout the length and breadth of Italy Cesare's name was spoken with a shudder. There are many stories concerning his lust and cruelty. There was an occasion when a young and beautiful girl, whom he desired and who had repulsed him, was on her way to her betrothal, when she was abducted by him to satisfy the lust of an hour.

He loved his mother throughout his life and she adored him; he was still the favourite of all her children; she readily forgave him the murder of her son Juan, as she did the sorrow he had brought to Lucrezia by murdering her husband. In Vannozza's eyes Cesare could do no wrong, for Cesare was superhuman. In exchange for this devotion, and perhaps for seeing him as he saw himself, he showered honours on his mother, making her one of the richest women in Italy, and visited her frequently.

His passionate love for Lucrezia persisted throughout his life as did hers for him and, when Lucrezia suffered a miscarriage and was under the influence of violent fever, Cesare hastened to her bedside that he might hold her foot while the leeches were applied and the blood-letting went on. It was Cesare's presence in her bedchamber which gave her a new desire to live, and during that melancholy time only he could cheer her, which, we are told, he usually did by telling her lewd stories.

Cesare's love for his mother and sister is not difficult to understand. Sadistic, callous as he was with all others, for these two he had an undying devotion. The reason was that they both saw him as more than a man; he was the most important person in their lives and, no matter what other loves they had, Cesare reigned supreme. For this devotion, for this estimate of him, which was his own, he repaid them by rare affection on his part.

For his father he had not the same devotion. It may have been that he never forgave Alexander, first for making Juan his favourite son, and secondly for insisting that he, Cesare, should enter the Church. It might have been that, had Alexander's position in the Vatican not been so important to Cesare's success, he would have revenged himself for these slights to his enormous pride and dignity.

There is one story of how, in the Pope's presence, Cesare lost his temper with one of the Cardinals and, unable to control his rage, took out a dagger and prepared to attack the Cardinal there in the presence of the Holy Father himself. Alexander sternly reproved his son for his conduct, but was sharply threatened that he had better take care lest the same dagger was used against him.

Alexander, determined to make light of his son's violent and increasingly alarming conduct, declared that Cesare was good-hearted but that he could not bear an insult. "For my part," he added, "I have always been forgiving."

Alexander spoke truthfully there. Considering the age in which he lived and the power which was his, he was often lenient with his enemies. But he does not escape the charge of complicity in the many poison plots which were concocted by his family.

*   *   *

In the August of 1503 the Borgia power was at its height. Cesare was master of Rome and ruled that city—and some said his father.

Then came that fatal day when the Pope and his son were invited to a party at the vineyard of Cardinal Adriano Castelli da Corneto. The party was to be held in the Cardinal's vineyard just outside the city.

It is not known what actually happened at that party, but it is clear that it was the beginning of disaster.

One story says that the Borgias were planning to murder the Cardinal because he was very wealthy and they wanted his estates. Into a jar of jam they proposed to introduce the notorious *cantarella* which was to be offered to the Cardinal. The Cardinal, however, knowing of the fate which was being prepared for him, persuaded the hired murderers to turn the tables and poison that food which was to be offered to Cesare and Alexander.

Whether that story is true or not, the fact remains that after that banquet Alexander and Cesare were violently ill. So, we are told, were others who attended the banquet. Corneto himself retired to bed, but whether he was actually ill or thought it wise to feign illness, is not known.

Several modern historians insist that the illness of Alexander and Cesare at this time was tertian fever; but most of the contemporary recorders are certain that Alexander and Cesare were poisoned; although Costabili wrote that many were ill of fever in Rome at that time owing to the pestilential air.

For days Cesare and Alexander were near death, and when they did not die immediately it was thought by some that their pact with the devil had saved them and that the Borgias had superhuman powers, and while they used their poisons to exterminate their enemies, the same weapon could not successfully be turned against themselves.

The Pope seemed to recover and was well enough to play cards with his family, but a few days later he had an apoplectic fit and it became clear this time that he could not survive.

He was calm on his death-bed; blithely and true to character, he refused to see that the life he had led was not entirely that which a Pope should lead; he forgot the lewdness, the incest, the murders; and serenely he allowed himself to drift out of this life with the certainty that as Christ's Vicar there would be a place of honour waiting for him in Heaven.

Rumour immediately declared that the devil had visited him at the end, demanding his soul in agreed payment for the Papacy, for the years of vigour equalling that of a young man, and for immunity from early death.

There was excitement throughout Italy. The Pope was dead, and the enemies of the Borgias prepared to come into their own. Cesare was very ill, confined to his bed at this moment when he should have been guarding with the utmost strength and caution all that he had won.

The physicians were with him, fighting to bring him back to life. He was in a raging fever so that he scarcely knew that the dire event had taken place. Those parts of his body which were swollen and discoloured were wrapped in the still warm entrails of a disembowelled mule and he was plunged into icy baths. The drastic treatment did not prevent his recovery from the fever, but its mark was left upon him and would remain for the rest of the life which was left to him.

He rose from his sick bed to realize that his enemies were demanding retribution. A few days after the death of Pope Alexander, Cesare was retiring to Castel Saint Angelo, there to seek refuge until it was safe for him to emerge.

*   *   *

That was the end of Cesare's glory. Enemies loomed on all sides. Louis, his one time ally, no longer found him useful, and promptly deserted him. The aged Cardinal Piccolomini was elected Pope Pius III, but he died after a reign of twenty-seven days, and Cesare's old enemy, Giuliano della Rovere was elected as Julius II.

Cesare had no friends except Lucrezia and Vannozza. In Ferrara, Lucrezia worked with all her might to save him from disaster. Vannozza would have done the same had she been

able. But Cesare's troops were to desert him, and he was to see
slip from his fingers all that he had gained. In vain did Lucrezia
write to the King of France begging that her brother might
be allowed to take up his estate in Valence; in vain did she
plead with those Cardinals whom she had believed to be her
father's friends.

Cesare was eventually made a prisoner and kept in that room
where Lucrezia's second husband, Alfonso of Bisceglie, had
been murdered by his orders. By all accounts, Cesare was not
in the least disturbed that this place should be chosen for him.
It seems to have been a family characteristic that there were no
regrets for the past. When a deed was done it was forgotten.
He was ready to forget all the cruelty he had inflicted on others
and seemed rather surprised that others were not. The only
thing he remembered was the insult to his pride. Now the
megalomaniac was frustrated and bewildered to learn how much
of his greatness had not come through himself but through his
father.

Alexander had died in August 1503 and it was not until
April 1504 that Cesare escaped from the prison in which della
Rovere had placed him, and arrived in Naples; but there, on
the orders of King Ferdinand he was made a prisoner and sent
to the island of Ischia.

He was kept there for two months until he agreed to surrender Romagna. He must have known ..en that all he had
gained was lost. A few days after he had signed the order for
surrender, he left for Spain.

There was not a very warm welcome waiting for him in
Spain. When she heard that he was coming, his sister-in-law,
Juan's widow, asked the King and Queen of Spain that her
husband's murderer should be brought to justice. The King and
Queen were ready to listen to her. They did not forget the
pro-French policy of the Borgias in later years and they were
of the opinion that it was Cesare who had persuaded his
father to this.

So exactly a year after his father's death, Cesare, who had
hoped to unite all Italy under his leadership was once more
a prisoner. This time his prison was the fortress of Cincilla, and
he must have felt that the future held no hope for him when
he heard that the King had decided he should stand his trial
for the murder of his brother.

But Cesare was not brought to trial. Low as he had fallen
he was still of some importance in the game of high politics, and
the Spanish King and Queen knew that, while Cesare Borgia
lived, Pope Julius was going to have some uneasy moments.

Cesare's melancholy frustration must have been complete during those months. Lucrezia continued to work for his freedom, and no doubt Vannozza to mourn for him.

It was not until near the end of the year 1506 that Cesare escaped from the prison, to which he had been transferred, in the castle of Medina del Campo, and reached Pamplona where he met his brother-in-law, the King of Navarre, who was engaged in war with the Count of Lerin.

He asked to be allowed to join his brother-in-law; permission was readily granted, and leading a hundred horse he went on ahead of his men and was surrounded by the enemy.

Terribly wounded, he was stripped and left naked to die. This happened on 12th March, 1507. He was between thirty and thirty-one years of age.

That was the end of Cesare, one of the most sadistic, brutal and notoriously evil men of any age.

LA MARQUISE DE BRINVILLIERS

SEVENTEENTH-CENTURY PARIS

THE REPUTATION of the Borgias lived on after them, and it was shared to some extent by the Medicis. The names of these two families immediately spring to the minds of most people when poison is mentioned; and there is no doubt that they were adepts at the art; it flourished under them because poisoning was a method of killing which appealed to their natures. Thus they were the founders of a dynasty of poisoners.

The best-known poison of the fifteenth and sixteenth centuries was arsenic, which formed the basis of the notorious Borgia poison *cantarella*. *Aqua toffana*, which is often associated with the Medicis, was believed to be a solution of arsenic together with a form of cantharides.

It was the Medicis who brought the fashion for poisoning into France. Perhaps this is one of the reasons why Catherine de' Medici and Marie de' Medici were so hated by the French, for it must have been noticed that soon after the arrival of each, a new terror swept over the land; and it was in France that the description '*Italien*' often carried with it an additional meaning: '*Empoisonneur.*'

When Catherine de' Medici came into France to marry the young Duc d'Orléans, who afterwards became Henri Deux, she brought with her, as was customary, a train of attendants. Among these were her *parfumeurs*, the makers of her cosmetics and her astrologers. The concoction of poisons was often carried on under the cloak of these respectable trades, and it was not long after Catherine's entry into France that mysterious deaths were taking place.

The most important in those days was that of Dauphin François, who, heated after playing tennis, asked for a cup of water, and when this was brought to him, drank it and immediately died. By his death Catherine's husband became Dauphin and later King; and it was not forgotten that the fatal draught was handed to François by his *Italien* cupbearer. The cupbearer was accused of poisoning the Dauphin (he confessed to this, but only after the Question Extraordinary was applied), and suffered a terrible death when his body was torn asunder by four wild horses, to each of which one of his limbs was attached. But it was Catherine de' Medici who was the instigator of the crime—so said the people of France.

It was also said that Catherine de' Medici's old enemy, the Cardinal of Lorraine, died after handling money which had been treated with a poison which penetrated the pores of the skin.

Catherine is suspected of hurrying to his death her son François that she might put Charles IX, over whom she had absolute control, on the throne; she is accused of poisoning Charles in favour of her beloved son, Henri III.

Indeed, almost all deaths which occurred in high places during the lifetime of Catherine de' Medici were alleged to be her work or that of her agents, the Ruggieri brothers and René, the Florentine who had his shop on the quay not far from the Louvre.

These were, there is no doubt, the creatures of Catherine, and much of the work which went on in the secret apartments behind their shops was concerned with experimenting with poisons such as could be found in the woods and meadows around Paris: water hemlock, foxgloves, henbane, and the prussic acid of the almond tree.

It is said that many of the poisons which were used with such effect in the fifteenth, sixteenth and seventeenth centuries were procured by methods which are today, most fortunately, unknown. There is no doubt that during those centuries poisoning was becoming an art practised by men and women of all classes, and was not necessarily used to bring about death. Not only did those who lived close to the Borgias and Catherine de' Medici suffer in this way. Richelieu suffered from many mysterious illnesses. So did Louis XIII, and of him it is said that his state of health deteriorated as his relationship with his mother—Marie de' Medici—did so.

There was experimenting with poisons which involved trying them out on people regarding whose life or death the poisoner must have been completely indifferent, as well as those doses which were given as a sharp lesson, a little rap over the knuckles as though to imply: 'This is a foretaste of what will happen if you do not behave well!'

In some circles it was customary every morning to take an antidote. Food was so highly spiced that it was impossible to detect alien flavours and one could have taken poison without having noticed it.

The effectiveness of ptomaine poisoning was discovered by these craftsmen, as is shown by one of the most famous of all poisons: *venin de crapaud*. To obtain this, arsenic was administered to various creatures—the toad being the favourite—and when they died, juices were distilled from their bodies. This proved to be a deadly poison, because not only was it composed of the virus of arsenic but all the attendant poisons of decomposition.

As in a previous century people had feared men such as the Ruggieri brothers and René the Florentine, so in the seventeenth century the most notorious maker of poisons was a certain Antonio Exili who was sometimes known as Eggidi.

He was an Italian and little is known of his origins or his end. He appeared in the capitals of Europe in the middle of the seventeenth century, and his name came to be spoken with awe and dread.

It was said of him that he knew more about poisons than any man living, and that he carried secrets which he sold dearly to the heads of states. He could supply death—it was said—in any form which was required: lingering death, quick death, painful death or death as gentle as sleep. It was accounted to him that he could foretell the hour, even if it were a month ahead, when a healthy man would cease to exist.

Rumour continued that he was hired by Olympia Maldachini, niece of Innocent X, who was very influential at the Papal Court; and he worked well for this woman so that she became very rich. The rumour continued that Olympia sold honours to certain men and, when the bargain was completed, with the subtle help of Exili they died. Then that particular post was once more vacant, and saleable by the unscrupulous Olympia.

This could not go on indefinitely and it became necessary for Exili to leave Italy. He then appeared in the service of the eccentric Christina of Sweden; and from Sweden he came to France.

The French were well aware of his record and not anxious to have him practising in their country; and when a difference arose between Sweden and France, Exili found that the protection of Christina was no longer of use to him. Because there was great fear of this man in French circles, he was taken to the Bastille, and as a result makes his appearance in the case of the Marquise de Brinvilliers.

*　　　*　　　*

Marie Marguerite d'Aubray, who on her marriage became the Marquise de Brinvilliers, was born, some say, in the year 1630, others 1634.

Marie was a beautiful girl; her hair was abundant and light brown in colour; her eyes were blue; she was bold, dainty, small and very ambitious. She wanted all the luxuries of the world and, because she was young, beautiful and of moderately good family, she did not see why she should not have them. She was sensual and frivolous, and determined from her earliest days to have what she wanted from life.

The d'Aubrays originally came from Lorraine and owned land in Picardy. Marie's father, Antoine Dreux d'Aubray, had decided that Paris offered him better opportunities to lead the life he wanted, and accordingly settled there. In the Capital he found the milieu he sought and became rich and important. As Seigneur of Offémont and Villiers, he held many posts, including that of Civil Lieutenant of the City of Paris. His duties in this respect brought him into contact with the police; he was a protégé of Jean Baptiste Colbert, himself a protégé of Mazarin and one of the most important of French ministers.

Monsieur d'Aubray was therefore in a position to arrange a good marriage for his eldest daughter, and his choice fell upon a dissolute young man who was not only Marquis de Brinvilliers but Baron de Nourar.

Marie was seventeen years old (if she were born in 1634) when the marriage took place. The second Fronde war was still in progress, and, living in Paris, she would have seen the effects of the Fronde wars—the Old Fronde, 1648 to 1649, and the New Fronde which did not end until a year after her marriage.

Such a war at such a time would have inevitably bred in a young person a certain lack of respect for life. As Cesare Borgia had, at an early age, she would have seen brutal fighting in the streets. This may have been instrumental in perverting her into the sort of woman she became; but it must have been that, from early days, that seed was in her nature as it was in that of Cesare. It grew into a simple philosophy: The lives of others are of no importance; that of Marie Marguerite d'Aubray is of supreme importance.

The married couple started their life together with the brightest prospects. Each was possessed of a fortune, for Monsieur d'Aubray gave with his daughter a handsome dowry, and the joint income of the pair was somewhere in the region of £40,000. In those days when the value of money was far greater than it is today, this was a great fortune. But they were both also possessed of extravagant tastes, and it was not long before they found this vast sum inadequate for their needs.

The foremost fashion which was sweeping the Court at this

time was gambling. Anne of Austria, indolent and pleasure-loving, was a devotee of the pastime, and the fashion raged throughout the Court. It was inevitable, therefore, that those living on the fringes of the Court should follow, and, once the craze started, it continued. Basset and lansquenet, hoca and ombre; they were played through the night and into the morning.

In the Hôtel d'Aubray, where the young couple had set up house together, there were card parties every night, and carriages were seen rumbling over the cobbles in the Rue Neuve Saint-Paul from early evening until after dawn.

The Marais in those days was one of the fashionable quarters of Paris and therein many of the highest nobles of France had their hôtels. This was so until the building of Versailles when the Marais began to deteriorate and the old hôtels were for-saken for others round about the Faubourg Saint-Germain or on the roads leading to Versailles.

The Hôtel d'Aubray was a most imposing dwelling with its courtyards and gardens and its many rooms, a fitting residence for people of such wealth and standing.

Unfortunately the Marquis had no intention of changing his mode of life on marriage; and it had always been a par-ticularly dissolute mode. The marriage must have been one of convenience—the parties were French—and no doubt he felt that as long as he lived occasionally with his wife and provided her with children, it was all that could be reasonably expected of him.

There were children of the marriage, but Marie was not the woman to content herself merely with a domestic life. The Marquis had his mistresses, and the favourite of all these was a Mademoiselle Dufay. Marie did not take exception to this state of affairs; she was a realist and she knew that most men had their mistresses; it was the custom of the country: a marri-age of convenience which would bring an adequate dowry and be the means of perpetuating the family name, that was duty; but there must be mistresses to minister to a man's pleasure.

Marie had never been in love with Brinvilliers and was glad to be rid of him, for his absences gave her a chance to lead her own life. Marie, on her own confession, was no virtuous wife. Why should she be? She had as much right to take her pleasure as her husband had. Marie took liberally.

She revelled in her beauty, adorning it with black patches of taffeta called *mouches*, which were so fashionable and becoming; she painted her face, dyed her hair and spent a great deal of time with her dressmaker. She took lovers and ran up her gambling debts.

Marie's father was a little concerned about his daughter's way of life and on several occasions warned her, but Marie could never endure criticism. She probably told herself that if she ran up debts she would find some means of paying them. If she lost one night, she might win the next.

Paris was growing gay again. The wars were over and Colbert was working hard to restore the country's prosperity. Louis XIV had thrown off the rule of his mother and Mazarin, and was determined to be King more than in name. He was often seen riding about the Capital, and wherever he appeared the people would cheer him. He possessed two qualities which endeared him to his subjects; he was good to look on in his youthful beauty and he was benign.

Louis in his state robes of purple decorated with the golden lilies, in his satin, velvet and ruffles, was certainly one of the handsomest Kings the French had ever had; young and healthy he excelled in the hunt and ballet; he lived in lavish splendour, and those who could wanted to follow the fashion set by the King.

Here was peace; here was prosperity. The theatres were as diverting as they had ever been. Molière was writing his plays for the amusement of the Court; Madeleine de Scudéry was writing her novels, and her brother Georges was writing his dramatic pieces. Racine had not yet arrived in Paris but would shortly do so. The literary scene was about to break out in a brilliance which even excelled that of the days of François Premier.

In Paris there were the literary circles—*les coteries précieuses*—such as Mademoiselle de Scudéry's famous *Samedi*, which was another Rambouillet, although on a smaller scale. Here wit abounded and artists rubbed shoulders with the wealthy, for the circle must be '*littéraire et galant*'.

But the Marquise de Brinvilliers, with her *mouches* and frivolities, would never have been accepted in such circles. She would have declared she had no wish to be admitted. She would no doubt have snapped her fingers at the blue-stockings who read their poetry to one another and discussed the Court with wit which was abundant and scathing.

No, the parties of the Marquise were very different from those of Madeleine de Scudéry. Marie's evenings provided the thrills of the card-table and *amours* to come.

And so these two were content to lead their own lives: the Marquis with his mistresses—chief among them Mademoiselle Dufay—and the Marquise with her parties and her lovers. The trouble was that both needed a great deal more money than they possessed; and they were mortgaging their future to pay for their immediate pleasures.

Both no doubt possessed the gambler's optimism. One day their luck would turn. One day the cards would be kind to them, luck would sit at their elbows and their lost fortunes would be retrieved.

Meanwhile Monsieur Antoine Dreux d'Aubray continued to warn his daughter; she listened quietly, one presumes; but she had no intention of reforming her ways. No doubt she told herself that her father was an old fool who did not realize that she was different from other people. *They* might run into difficulties; not so Marie Marguerite de Brinvilliers. She had the gift of seeing herself supreme; she was not going to change her mode of life simply because she had had bad luck at the card tables.

Marie was the eldest of the family. She had two brothers and a sister who had become a Carmelite nun; and when her father died she would share his fortune with them; so, if she were to continue her reckless extravagant way of life, she might be temporarily embarrassed, but there was hope of possessing more wealth in the future.

She smiled tolerantly at her father. Perhaps she implied that he had been listening to evil tales of her life. He was not to worry about her. She knew very well how to take care of herself.

Antoine would have gone away, perhaps a little comforted. He would know it was true that Marie had always known how to take care of herself.

*   *   *

Marie's husband, Antoine Gobelin de Brinvilliers, came from a family which has been called *parvenu*. As sometimes happens in such a family, the wealth of which has been built up by shrewd business ability and good industry, there appears one member who is dissolute and of quite different character from the founders of his name and fortune.

It may have been that Antoine Gobelin had been born into luxury and had never had to work for his living, as his forbears had, and that this made him the careless spendthrift that he was. He accepted luxury as his right and, because it had always been his, he believed it always would be, and therefore was lazy and recklessly extravagant.

The Gobelins originally came from Flanders and established their works on the banks of La Bièvre which flowed through a section of Paris. So beautiful were their dyes that they became famous and, as they kept the process a secret and no one had ever seen such colours before, it was said that the goblins worked for them during the night, for such colours could not have been produced by man alone. Thus, in the first instance they received their name.

At this time the family were merely dyers and had not yet opened the tapestry factory, although before 1700 they ceased to be dyers and had given themselves up completely to the production of tapestry.

If his hard-working ancestors would have scorned the Marquis, much he cared. He was only intent on having a good time; and it was when he was racketing about Paris in search of it, that he made the acquaintance of Gaudin de Sainte-Croix.

Sainte-Croix was a Captain in the Cavalry when he made the acquaintance of Brinvilliers. He was a native of Gascony and there was a secret surrounding his birth. Some authorities state that he was the illegitimate son of a person of such high rank that he could not claim the relationship. Whether this is true or not it is impossible to state. It may have been one of the stories which Sainte-Croix delighted to circulate about himself.

He had all the confidence and the recklessness of a Gascon, and the Gascons were declared to be the most arrogant and the most mischievous of men.

He was very handsome, highly intelligent and alert; he had the gift of adjusting his manners to his company so that he was as much at home with priests as with vagabonds. He was completely without scruples and was ready to enter into any plot which offered profit or excitement; his love affairs were numerous; yet it amused him to mingle with the religious and assume a sanctimonious attitude, and this he did so well that he almost believed in his sincerity. He was a man of great charm, and irresistible to most women with whom he came into contact.

Antoine de Brinvilliers was immediately attracted by him, as perhaps Sainte-Croix had intended he should be. Sainte-Croix was invariably in a state of impecuniosity, for his tastes were extravagant, and the young Marquis would appear to him to be a man of wealth; therefore Sainte-Croix would not have been himself if he had not sought to exploit the situation.

For some months they were continually together; Sainte-Croix won money from the Marquis; they visited low taverns together and shared amorous adventures. Sainte-Croix became for the Marquis the perfect companion, rumbustious, witty, all that was demanded, just as when his companions had been of a religious turn of mind, Sainte-Croix had quoted the Scriptures.

Sainte-Croix, full of vigour, determined to get what he could from life and enjoy every minute of it.

After some months of friendship, the Marquis took Sainte-Croix to the Hôtel d'Aubray.

Some say that the Marquis took Sainte-Croix to his home for the purpose of supplying his wife with a lover, because he, the Marquis, wanted to be free to conduct his own *amours*.

This seems hardly likely, for both the Marquis and Madame de Brinvilliers had been living their own lives for some years. It is unlikely that Marie would have cared where a husband, to whom she was indifferent, spent his time. She had her lovers; she would not grudge her husband his.

I think it is possible that the Marquis took his friend to his home because it was convenient and natural to do so.

The inevitable happened.

Madame de Brinvilliers could never in her life have met a man so charming as the fascinating Gascon.

Sainte-Croix doubtless had heard something of her from her husband or, if not from him, from other sources. He was the type who liked to plot, and it is possible that he planned to make Madame de Brinvilliers his mistress as soon as possible, and had already adapted his personality to suit the woman he understood her to be.

He was very successful. Within a very short time, Marie was recklessly in love with Sainte-Croix.

*   *   *

Sainte-Croix was so frequently at the Hôtel d'Aubray that it might be said he lived there. The Marquis appears to have implied that he had no objection. Sainte-Croix had transferred his friendship from the husband to the wife. The Marquis was content with Mademoiselle Dufay to whom he had remained constant far longer than to any of his other mistresses.

The Marquise was hardly ever seen at functions without Sainte-Croix and they would be observed leaving the house in her carriage in the afternoons and returning to it, after parties, in the early mornings.

The Gascon, as an adventurer, was fully aware that his prospects had never been so good.

There was soon scandal about what was happening at the Hôtel d'Aubray and Marie was brought to book by her family. She snapped her fingers at them—father and brothers. They could live their own lives the way they wanted to, she said; she would live hers as she liked.

Meanwhile scandal persisted, and this state of affairs existed for two years. But during this time the gambling debts of Marie and her husband had so increased that their fortune was rapidly diminishing. Sainte-Croix began to be worried. He was enjoying very much the comfortable existence of a member of the nobility, and he did not want anything changed. He knew how to charm his mistress, and she was as much in love with him as she had been during the first weeks of their passion. If, however, there was not enough money to go on living this idyllic existence, Sainte-Croix was going to be very disappointed. Accordingly he began to plan.

The Marquis was gambling more heavily than his wife and was squandering a great deal of money on his mistresses; and Sainte-Croix pointed out to Marie that, as their fortunes had been amalgamated, it was in her interest to take steps to have those fortunes separated. Then she could see to it that it was not her money with which the Marquis was not only paying some of his gambling debts but supporting his mistresses in luxury.

Marie immediately saw the point of this and began to institute proceedings.

Notice of this reached her brothers, and they were horrified. They knew that she was completely under the spell of the Gascon adventurer, and they felt that if Marie attempted to separate her fortune from her husband's she might bring trouble on her head. She knew nothing of the law; as for Sainte-Croix, he was a law unto himself. Those two did not realize what they were attempting to do.

Marie's brothers called on her and remonstrated with her. Marie was infuriated by their interference and told them so. They then decided that there was only one thing to do, and that was to inform their father of what was happening at the Hôtel d'Aubray. He alone, they decided, could bring that infatuated woman to her senses. She must take notice of what her father said, for, if she flouted him, he would surely cut her out of his will.

When her father arrived at the hôtel in Rue Neuve Saint-Paul, Marie's anger against her brothers was unbounded; she was furious at her father's interference also, but Marie could curb her anger when it was expedient to do so.

She dared not talk to her father as she had to her brothers, so she listened while he told her she was a fool. Did she not realize that he, as Civil Lieutenant of the City of Paris, knew more of the law than she did? He visualized her losing the whole of her fortune; and what would be more understandable if, in view of her conduct, her husband disowned her? Then she and her children would be forced to come begging to him!

Marie refused to be impressed. He implored her to put a stop to her liaison with Sainte-Croix. The high-spirited Marie

would surely have reminded him of her husband's *affaire* with
Mademoiselle Dufay. He would patiently explain that *that*
was different. There was one law for men, another for women.

But Marie had decided that this was not going to be the case
with the Marquise de Brinvilliers. Let her husband take his
mistresses; that did not worry her, provided she had her lovers
and was not expected to help pay for her husband's extrava-
gances.

Antoine Dreux d'Aubray reminded his daughter that, in his
position as Civil Lieutenant, it would not be difficult for him
to put a stop to his daughter's way of life.

Marie clearly did not take this threat seriously, but Monsieur
d'Aubray must have been enraged when he left her, because he
immediately applied to Louis himself, through his friends in
high places, for a *lettre de cachet* against the adventurer, Sainte-
Croix.

These *lettres de cachet* were much feared throughout France.
They were warrants of imprisonment sealed with the King's
private seal, and, on receipt of one, the person whom the
order concerned would be conveyed to prison. He or she would
be given no explanation or reason; the whole matter was secret.
It was merely the King's wish that that person should be
withdrawn from society, and so it was done. Families quite
frequently applied for these sealed letters and, if they had
friends in the right quarter, these were not withheld.

The receiver of a *lettre de cachet* was not necessarily a criminal,
but merely a person who must prepare himself or herself to be
incarcerated during the King's pleasure.

Fathers, with sons or daughters whom they feared might bring
dishonour to the family would ask for a *lettre de cachet* so that
the recalcitrant offspring might cool his or her heels in cap-
tivity.

There is no doubt that these *lettres de cachet* were responsible
for a great deal of cruelty and injustice; and the practice was a
barbarous one; but it continued until 1790.

As the result of the action of Marie's father, Sainte-Croix
was arrested one day, when he was leaving the Hôtel d'Aubray,
and taken to the Bastille.

When she knew that her lover had been imprisoned because
of the action of her father, Marie was extremely wrathful.
She hated her family, and she must have longed to tell them so.
But she did no such thing. The hatred within her was allowed
to smoulder; and the more she missed her lover, the greater
that hatred grew. It may have been that then she began to
ponder and realize that, if they were all dead, the vast family

fortune would be hers. She would not miss *them*, and what good use she could make of the money!

* * *

Life in the Bastille during the reign of Louis XIV was not always so hideous as it is often believed to have been. Many of the prisoners, such as those in the position of Sainte-Croix, who had not been incarcerated because of criminal acts but because he was proving himself to be a nuisance in the family of a man of influence, enjoyed a considerable amount of freedom.

They were allowed to exercise in the courtyards, to meet others of their kind, and even to entertain their friends. They entered into discussions, played games, and, in fact, lived moderately well; the principal hardship was that they were not allowed to leave the precincts of the Bastille.

Their relations, who had put them under restraint, invariably contributed to their keep, and if they came from wealthy families this meant that they lived in comparative ease. It is likely that Monsieur d'Aubray contributed to the expenses of Sainte-Croix (and Marie certainly would) and it is obvious that he enjoyed certain privileges while in the Bastille, for Monsieur d'Aubray was no tyrant, and, in arranging for the imprisonment of his daughter's lover, his one aim had been to deliver her from this man's disastrous influence.

Sainte-Croix's feelings, as the coach carried him through the streets towards the great fortress, must have been murderous, for it was well known that once a man entered the Bastille he never knew when he would be released. No doubt he imagined what would happen if he were held prisoner for any great length of time. Marie would surely find herself another lover and his plans for an easy life would never fructify.

As the coach lumbered along and drew near to the prison, the people in the streets would be alert. They would see in what direction the coach was going. Another prisoner taken to the Bastille!

It was a forbidding place, the great Bastille, with its eight pointed towers, surrounded by a moat which was only filled when the Seine overflowed its banks. It dominated the Rue Saint-Antoine and passers-by could see the heavy doors and the enormous locks; they must have shuddered, for there had always been gruesome stories connected with the Bastille, more than with any other Paris prison. People talked of the dungeons—the *cachots*—dark and dank, the floors of which were covered in slime, and which gave off pestilential air and were the home of rats and reptiles; the *chambres rigoureuses* were nothing more than iron cages placed immediately above the dungeons; these were about six feet square, and in them men and women were shut away until they died. There were the terrifying *oubliettes* reputed to be fitted with a contrivance of wheels which drew the victim to it and, when he was caught, cut him to pieces. There were the *calottes* which were built in the summit of the towers and so shaped that the prisoner could stand upright only when he was in the centre of the cell. Scarcely any light came through to these *calottes*, and, because of their position, the heat in the summer was intense, and the cold in the winter unbearable. There was talk of one room which was lighted with numerous candles and decorated with flowers, the scent of which was overpoweringly lovely to a prisoner who had been shut away in a dank dungeon with rats for company. It is said that this was additional torture fabricated by men who gave their time to planning new and more exquisite tortures, and that prisoners were taken to this room and promised their liberty. When they were ready to swoon with joy and on their knees in gratitude, the floor would suddenly open and the wretched prisoner would endure a second or so of intense horror which seemed like eternity, while he looked down at the wheel of knives in the *oubliette* below him, and on to which he was about to fall. These matters were talked of by the shuddering citizens as they passed the great Bastille.

The Bastille was the home of legend. But Mercier says that the people dreaded the Châtelet more than the Bastille. This may have been due to the fact that the poor and the unimportant were not taken to the Bastille which was ironically called the *Hôtel des Gens de Lettres*.

The legends concerning the Bastille have been given long life by writers who used these for dramatic effect; and there is strong suspicion that they have been exaggerated out of all proportion to the truth.

Sainte-Croix would, therefore, have been allowed to walk in the courtyards, to read, chat, or even keep a pet. There is no record that he kept pets, but others did, and among these pets were carrier pigeons which could be put to useful purpose.

Some prisoners were allowed to walk on the ramparts, when they could look down on the Rue Saint-Antoine and the Rue Saint-Paul. If their friends knew the hour at which they would be allowed to do this the friends could take their stand in these streets and signal. Messages wrapped round stones were said to have been flung from across the moat in the hope that people who picked them up might deliver them to the person to whom they were addressed.

So the prisoner who was detained for family reasons very often lived well and was not entirely cut off from the world; and it was during his six weeks' incarceration in the Bastille that Sainte-Croix met the man who was going to have such an influence on his life and that of Madame de Brinvilliers. This was Exili, the Italian professional poisoner who was being detained in the Bastille because he was a person who threatened the security of people in high places.

Sainte-Croix had dabbled in chemistry, but there was nothing unusual in this, for there was hardly a man in Europe who, providing he had the means, would not have embarked on a series of chemical experiments. The desires of people of those days were much the same as they are today, and there were two possessions for which they longed more than any others: health and wealth. So, in laboratories all over Europe, experiments were being made in the hope of discovering the two means of satisfying these desires: the Philosopher's Stone which, it was believed, would transmute base metals into gold or silver and so provide the wealth; and the Elixir of Life which would be the means of living for ever. Therefore it was not surprising that a man such as Sainte-Croix should have made his attempts to discover these two, since almost every man of some education was doing the same.

Sainte-Croix must have been delighted to make the acquaintance of a man so notorious as Exili, and as they walked together in the courtyards of the Bastille no doubt told the professional poisoner of his experiments and asked his opinion.

Exili, one imagines, laughed at those who searched vainly for the Philosopher's Stone or the Elixir of Life. Perhaps he reminded his new friend that men had searched for these elusive benefits for centuries and that, although a great deal of time and money had been spent in the search, no one had come near to finding them.

But, in the course of their experiments, men had made other discoveries. Exili was one of these men. And so exciting—so profitable—had been these discoveries, that he had at length ceased to concern himself with searching for what might well be the non-existent; yet he had made a name for himself and a great deal of money by his discoveries in other directions.

It was seen, such was his reputation, that almost as soon as the ministers of Louis XIV had been able to do so, they had put him under restraint. They feared Exili as they had feared few men.

It must have been that Sainte-Croix nourished this friendship. One imagines his using all his charm, which was considerable, to win the confidence of this man. Plans would be forming in his volatile mind which must always have plans to work on—whether good or bad plans, it was not of great importance—and at the moment he had his future to think of.

So he would have listened to Exili, who no doubt could not resist boasting of his skill; and it must have occurred to this adventurer from Gascony that a man would have great power over his fellow men if he could deal out death by some secret and mysterious means whenever he wished.

It may have been that he told Exili of the rage he felt over the action of Antoine Dreux d'Aubray, and how angered he had been that a man should have the power to place him under restraint, merely because he interfered with his peace of mind.

Exili was a professional poisoner; his secrets were for sale.

Sainte-Croix must have determined on getting the money to buy those secrets.

*　　　　*　　　　*

Antoine Dreux d'Aubray was undoubtedly a kindly man. He had meant that incarceration in the Bastille to be a lesson to his daughter and her lover; but he understood neither his daughter nor her lover.

After a period of six weeks, d'Aubray arranged that Sainte-Croix should be freed, and the Gascon went to the Hôtel d'Aubray immediately after his release. One imagines their passionate reunion, after which they would have reviled the man who had been responsible for the six weeks' separation.

Marie's character, as was later revealed, was a complex one. While Sainte-Croix was in prison she must have been working up a violent anger against, not only her father, but her brothers who had forced him to take the action he had. The fact that her father had her good at heart would count for nothing with Marie. She, who saw herself as of supreme importance, had been treated like a little girl whose favourite toy is taken from her because an adult thinks it may not be good for her. Marie was determined to show her family that she was not a little girl, and that no one could treat her as such with impunity.

Marie would have determined on revenge and Sainte-Croix concurred. But it must be complete revenge, and conversations with Exili would have taught Sainte-Croix that they had a good deal to learn.

They must not take their revenge in a clumsy manner which would be obvious to all those about them. He would probably have told her of his friendship with Exili, and that the notorious Italian, knowledgeable as he was, continued to experiment; he

spent all his time—when he was not in prison—experimenting;
yet he was a master of the art of poisoning, and this had
brought him great power and wealth. Marie and Sainte-Croix
would surely be envious of a man whose very name could strike
terror into all those who came into contact with him. If Marie
and Sainte-Croix had had such a reputation, would Antoine
Dreux d'Aubray have dared to separate them?

It would be necessary, Sainte-Croix would have told her, to
buy those secrets which Exili was ready to sell. More than that
—why should they not discover new secrets?

Exili was seeking to discover some of the lost secrets of the
Borgias and the Medicis. The Borgias had had a poison which
enabled them to kill at will, it was said. They decided that a
man should die in a day . . . in a year . . . and he did so.

Jeanne of Navarre, it was said, had died merely by drawing
on a pair of gloves sold to her by Catherine de' Medici's
favourite poisoner, René the Florentine.

Such arts, it seemed, were lost; and the methods of the
seventeenth century were clumsy when compared with those of
the fifteenth and sixteenth.

Yet, if rumour was to be believed, the basis of the Borgia
and Medici poisons was arsenic; and that was easily obtainable.
It was possible to buy it in any apothecary's shop in the city of
Paris. One merely asked for '*Mort aux rats*', and arsenic was
handed over without demur.

Why should they not experiment as Exili was experimenting?
Why should they not enjoy the power of dealing death to their
enemies?

Marie was clearly fascinated. She was determined that she
was going to take her revenge on the man who had treated her
and her lover so slightingly.

What more complete revenge could there be than murder?

*   *   *

Sainte-Croix had been sent to the Bastille in March 1663;
in May of the same year he was free.

It is hardly likely that he could have intended to lead a quiet
and respectable life when he came out of the Bastille, but, to
the casual observer, it appeared that this was what he was
attempting to do.

It is not known whether all the plans he and Marie finally
put into execution were fabricated at that time, or whether one
grew out of another. It may have been that they had decided
on the murder of Marie's father and were perfecting their plans
during the next three years. It may also have been that they

had hoped to commit this crime much earlier, and would
have done so if they had had the help they had expected from
Exili.

Exili remained in the Bastille after Sainte-Croix was freed,
but there is no doubt that someone who was interested in
Exili—perhaps Queen Christina herself—was making efforts to
bring about his release.

Sainte-Croix and Marie would need money for their experiments, and more money to pay Exili for his secrets. How were
they to obtain this? Financial matters at the Hôtel d'Aubray
were not flourishing, and this would have been an added
incentive to commit the crime. Antoine Dreux d'Aubray was a
rich man, and when he died his fortune would be divided
amongst his children—and Marie would get her share.

She wanted the money immediately—revenge was secondary.

It may have been that Sainte-Croix and Marie decided that
the renewal of their *affaire* should be kept secret from her family
as they wanted no more trouble from Antoine. The powerful
Lieutenant of the City had shown them that he could send
either of them to prison if he wished. That short spell in the
Bastille was—as it had been meant to be—a warning. It must
not happen again.

So Sainte-Croix decided that, outwardly, he would lead a
respectable life. He hit on the idea of marrying. This would
throw the d'Aubrays right off the scent; it may also have been
that the lady whom he married brought him some fortune.
She was a quiet woman and must have been completely
overshadowed by her husband and the bold Marquise de
Brinvilliers. That is understandable. From all accounts Sainte-
Croix was a most attractive man; he was almost certain to have
been a very plausible one too.

Sainte-Croix was now able to set up in his own house and
surround himself with servants. One of these was the villainous
Jean Hamelin who was known as La Chaussée.

One of the rooms in the new house was made into a laboratory, and here Sainte-Croix was going to conduct his experiments. It may have been that he had arranged that, when
Exili came out of the Bastille, he would take the poisoner into
his house and gradually wheedle out of him those secrets which
he wished to possess.

He no longer gambled; he even went regularly to church; and
as his visits to Marie were very secret, all those who had known
him before his imprisonment were astonished at the change in
him.

That he should be so interested in his laboratory surprised

none. He was merely working for the discovery of the Philosopher's Stone and the Elixir of Life, as were so many others.

Exili was released from the Bastille at the end of June, only a few weeks after Sainte-Croix, but he was unable to stay in Sainte-Croix's house because the terms of his release were that he should leave France immediately.

There may have been time for a meeting between the two who had been prisoners together, but it would have been only a brief one. Although Madame d'Aubray, the wife of Marie's elder brother, declared that Exili lived for a while in the house of Sainte-Croix, there is a letter written by Desgrez—that indefatigable and most trustworthy agent of the police—to the effect that he conducted Exili to Calais and saw him leave for England on the 1st July.

So the meeting between Sainte-Croix and Exili after the latter's release may not have taken place at all; and it is probably due to this fact—or that the meeting was a very short one—that Sainte-Croix and Marie took so long to prepare the revenge they were to take on Monsieur d'Aubray. Nevertheless Exili must have given Sainte-Croix some advice, and it was probably through the Italian that Sainte-Croix got into touch with Christopher Glaser, one of the cleverest chemists in Paris.

At all events, the experiments had begun.

*   *   *

Christopher Glaser was one of the most well-known chemists of the age. He was a native of Switzerland and he had left that country hoping to find his fortune in Paris, where there doubtless seemed more opportunities than in his native Basle.

He was very clever, and his cleverness did not go unrecognized. He was continually experimenting, and had made several useful discoveries. He was noticed by the Court and given work under Vallot, who was physician to Anne of Austria, the Queen Mother. Louis put him in charge of the Jardin des Plantes, and eventually he became chemist to Louis himself and tutored Philippe—Louis' brother—in chemistry. He had written books on his subject and, at the time he made the acquaintance of Sainte-Croix, was a man of means.

In spite of his Court duties he kept on his establishment in the Rue du Petit-Lion in the Faubourg Sainte-Germain, above which was the sign '*Au Basilisk*' and an effigy of a serpent which had been copied from a book by the great Huguenot surgeon, Ambrose Paré. He was noted for his antidotes to poison which were much in demand and which he distilled himself and the manufacture of which was his secret. The favourite of these

was theriac, which was said to contain numerous drugs
including opium. Orviétan, brought into the country from
Orvieto, was another, and although the best antidote was
believed to be milk in large quantities, many people of rank
bought Glaser's remedies and took them regularly in case someone had seen fit to slip a dose of poison into their food or drink.

It is possible that Exili, unable to give Sainte-Croix the
help he had promised, introduced him to Glaser; and the
chemist eventually agreed to assist Sainte-Croix in his schemes.

Sainte-Croix took a room in the house of a widow in the
Place Maubert, then an overcrowded district of unsavoury
reputation although it was in the shadow of Notre Dame.

His own house was in the Rue des Bernardins—between the
Panthéon and the Seine. In those days this was almost on
the edge of the City. On the left bank of the Seine, opposite
the back of Notre Dame, it was then a very quiet thoroughfare
dominated by the Monastery of Saint Bernard.

But it was in this little room in the Place Maubert that
Sainte-Croix was spending most of his time. Here Christopher
Glaser joined him, and they worked together. It says a good
deal for the persuasive powers, or perhaps the charm, of
Sainte-Croix that Glaser consented to work with him. It is
difficult to understand Glaser. He was a man of growing
reputation and attached to the Court; he was making his way
in the world. It seems strange that he should have been prepared to give so much of his time to the sort of work Sainte-
Croix was doing.

It may have been that Sainte-Croix seduced the man from
his legitimate business with promises of great wealth; but the
fact remains that Glaser was prepared to work for long hours
in that little room which Sainte-Croix rented from the widow;
and together they must have sought to discover—or rediscover
—those subtle poisons which they believed were used by the
Borgias and the Medicis who had kept their secrets from the
world.

Glaser was clearly an ambitious man. He believed firmly in
the power of money; and if he could prove those old methods
to be more than legends, and if he could give tangible proof
of his discoveries, he must become a rich man, for there were
many people of importance in France who were ready to pay
handsomely for a means of removing their rivals and their
enemies in such a mysterious way that no one would attach
blame to them.

Marie must have eagerly watched for the results of the experiments. She was desperately in need of money, and greatly

desired to be in possession of that portion of her father's wealth which was going to help her out of her financial troubles.

But without Exili the work progressed slowly, and the great difficulty of testing the poisons soon arose.

Here was a concoction which they knew to be deadly; but how could they be certain what effect it would have on a human being? This thing had to be planned carefully. They must make sure that they had produced a poison which could not be easily discovered after a victim's death; for Marie knew that if her father died in mysterious circumstances her family would be almost certain to wonder whether she had had a hand in his destruction. Since they had all discussed the scandalous life she had led, they would be very ready to suspect her.

Then Marie decided on a plan for testing the poisons. To Sainte-Croix it seemed a brilliant one.

As, since Sainte-Croix's return from the Bastille, Marie and he had pretended to mend their ways, it did not seem strange that Marie should go regularly to the hospital, a basket of food on her arm, to visit the poor sick people.

Marie was often seen setting out from the Hôtel d'Aubray for the great hospital, Hôtel Dieu, which was between the Palais de Justice and Notre Dame. It might be wondered why she did not take her servant with her to carry the basket, or even send her servant to the hospital with the good things for those poor suffering people. But no! Marie's reformation was complete. Humbly in the role of *sainte fille* she would go herself.

Her father must have been delighted. His daughter was at last behaving with the decorum he would wish to see in a daughter of his. He liked to hear that she had been seen on her way to the hospital. He did not know that a solution of arsenic had been stirred into the wine she took to the patients, or that the food had been sprinkled with a powder which Sainte-Croix had prepared for her.

If Marie's desire for revenge on her family, if her need for money is understandable, her conduct at the Hôtel Dieu seems cold-blooded to such a degree as to be almost incredible. But it gives, I think, the real clue to her character. Those sick and suffering people were of so little account in her opinion that they were nothing but a means of helping her to carry out her experiments. How could she have gone into that dreary room of pain and added to the sufferings of the people she found there? When Louis XVI visited the Hôtel Dieu he was horrified by the conditions he found there, and this was more than a hundred years later; he found six, or even more, patients, crowded into one bed; those with contagious diseases mingled with the rest of the patients, and the dead were often left lying in beds with the living because there was not enough staff to attend to them. Marie must have found even worse conditions, for it is reasonable to suppose that conditions improved, if only slightly, during a hundred years. Yet, so callous was she, that she had no compunction in adding to the sufferings of these wretched people. She could only do this because she considered them of no importance whatever. She was ready to inflict horrible suffering and death on other human beings merely that she and Sainte-Croix might discover whether there was too much or too little deadly arsenic in their concoctions.

Marie was methodical in her work. She took a good note of the patients to whom she gave the food which had been carefully treated. "Come, my good friend," she would say. "Eat now." For she must be sure that the particular patient she selected actually ate the food; that was necessary to the experiment. She would watch the effect and ask anxiously if the poor creature had enjoyed it. Was the flavour good? And so on.

Reassured she would go home with her empty basket, and the next day would be again at the hospital—such an indefatigable sister of mercy—with more food in her basket.

Perhaps she would be told: Poor so-and-so died in the night. She would show great sympathy and ask after the manner of dying. It might be that she would ask to be taken to the *Salle des Cadavres* that she might take one last look at poor dear such-and-such in whom she had taken such an interest. Imagine her in that ghastly room with its one lamp hanging from the ceiling; it would be dark and damp, for the Seine washed the wall on one side as it was below the level of the river. There would be the bodies be, some lying on the marble slabs merely covered by coarse sheets, others in rough canvas wrappers waiting to be taken to the Clamart or one of the Paris medical schools, that the students and doctors might use them in their studies.

It is hardly likely that Marie, even then, felt any horror, so certain would she have been that these people—in fact all people—were merely in the world to serve Marie d'Aubray, Marquise de Brinvilliers.

Using the hospital in this manner was a far safer way of testing the experiments than practising on the servants. Servants were notoriously inquisitive, and there might have been some to connect mysterious sickness and death in the household with that secret room of Sainte-Croix's in the Place Maubert to which Madame de Brinvilliers went so frequently.

* * *

So she continued, the sister of mercy, taking little comforts, wine and dainty food to the patients of the Hôtel Dieu. Many of the ladies went to the hospital in masks, which was looked upon as a sign of humility as they wished to do their good deeds in secret. Marie decided that it would serve her purpose very well if she were as modest as the others. She mingled with them, proffering the food and drink, and if there appeared to be an even greater number of deaths than usual, and many more died in acute agony, the hospital staff would have told themselves—if they had thought it worth while remarking on it —that it was to be expected in a hospital.

There were still many experiments to be made.

We hear that Marie gave gooseberries, which she had very slightly treated with poison, to one of her maids, and immediately afterwards the girl was ill, but not seriously so. Another maid was very ill indeed after eating meat which Marie had given her. But it was clear that the best method of trying out the experiments was on the hospital patients.

They were very useful, these experiments, for Antoine Dreux d'Aubray was no fool, nor were his sons; and since the coming of Exili to Paris, the fear of poison had increased alarmingly.

There must be no suspicion attached to Marie and Sainte-Croix when the time came for the deed to be done. Thus the experiments were very necessary. So Marie went back and back again to the hospital.

*   *   *

Thus three years passed, after Sainte-Croix's release from the Bastille, before they were ready.

They then had what they called 'Glaser's Receipt' which would enable them to slip a draught into a goblet of wine and scarcely alter the taste of the wine; if the dose were large enough it would quickly produce death, while if it were smaller the effect would not be fatal. This was important, as it was necessary for it to appear that Monsieur d'Aubray was suffering from a prolonged illness, so that he must have several attacks before he died.

Everything was planned with care.

Months before the appointed time for committing the murder, Marie had become completely reconciled with her father. He was then delighted with his daughter. It must not be forgotten that Marie was a good-looking woman; she was dainty, *petite*, and with her white skin and blue eyes, very attractive. Her sister was a Carmelite, and it is certain that the Civil Lieutenant of the City was charmed by this more worldly daughter who, having run wild, had, it seemed to him, settled down to a life of sobriety.

They were, so he thought, the best of friends.

Marie must have been a cold and calculating person to deceive her father in this way. For months she had to play the devoted daughter and presumably did it with a convincing charm. She could not have seen him as the kindly parent, the man who had acted as he did, purely out of anxiety for her welfare. Of course Marie did not see him in that way, for she scarcely saw him at all. She saw only herself, her needs and her desires.

She was visiting her father frequently and there is no doubt that she allowed him to believe that she had given up Sainte-Croix. He would deplore the continued dissipation of her husband and be ready to make excuses for his daughter.

It was while she was staying with him in his Paris home that he began to be troubled by bouts of illness, and he eventually decided that a little rest in the country would do him good; so he went to his estate at Offémont in Picardy in the Compiègne area.

When he had been there for a little while he asked Marie if she would come and relieve him of his loneliness. He knew that she could not be very happy in the Hôtel d'Aubray where her husband showed no sign of reforming his ways, and he probably thought she would enjoy a little change.

Marie did not hurry. She probably reminded him that she had her duties in Paris; he must not forget that she had her children to care for. But she let him know, after a short hesitation, that she had decided there were enough servants in the Hôtel d'Aubray to attend to matters there. The children were in the best of health; he was not, and he was her father; therefore he should have first claim upon her.

So she went, and it is certain that she took with her a small packet which would have come from the little room in the Place Maubert.

Her father would have been delighted to see her, and she would have been ready to give him the pleasure of her company, attentive and dutiful, always considering how best to please him.

Alas, his health did not improve in the country but grew alarmingly worse. So bad was it that Monsieur d'Aubray, feeling himself to be near death, decided he must return to Paris and put his affairs in order. Soon after he came back to the Capital he was dead.

* * *

At last Marie had been able to watch the effect of Glaser's Receipt at close quarters, and she had come to the conclusion that in making the poison palatable much of its potency had been destroyed. It had been necessary to administer it twenty-seven times before the desired effect was reached.

The deaths of all prominent people at this time were suspected of being caused by poison, so naturally there was a suspicion that the Civil Lieutenant's death was also due to this cause, and there was an autopsy.

The verdict must have filled Marie and Sainte-Croix with exultation, for the doctors stated that Monsieur d'Aubray had died from natural causes.

The result of the autopsy had a marked effect on Marie. The true malignancy of her character began to emerge. Within her grasp was that secret which could give her power over life and death. She must have felt omnipotent. As for the doctors, she would consider them ignorant. That showed the worth of doctors! she would reason. Or rather did it show the power which was being generated in a little room on the Place Maubert.

She threw restraint aside. There was now no need to pretend, for her father who had imposed that need was dead.

Her life ran far from smoothly however. Now that the deed had been accomplished, she had time to look about her and see what was happening. She discovered that Sainte-Croix was unfaithful to her.

The only person in the world, other than herself, about whom she cared was Sainte-Croix. He maintained his fascination over her; but since he was not content with her alone they quarrelled furiously; she, therefore, determined to show him that she could match his infidelity with her own. She took a few lovers, including the Marquis de Nadaillac, a cousin of her husband. It was no use though; she still hankered after the adventurer Sainte-Croix.

She had five children, two of whom she believed to be Sainte-Croix's, but she cared little for them. She was ambitious, up to a point, for the boys, but one of the girls was so plain and dull that she despised her. In any case, she was not a maternally-minded woman; she was sensual and wanted the thrill of *amours* and gambling; she was extremely extravagant, and now that she had her share of her father's money, she was as reckless as she had ever been. The gambling parties began again.

She was up until dawn and never rose until the afternoon. One day Mademoiselle Dufay came to the house to see the

Marquis and, in a sudden fury, Marie took up a knife and tried to stab her husband's mistress. It was not that she cared about the Marquis' liaison with the woman; it was merely a sudden anger because her power to enslave all men had been openly challenged.

It may have been that she had been playing the restrained matron, the sister of mercy at the Hôtel Dieu too long.

Her character seemed to change from one extreme to another; and thus it was throughout her violent life.

It was very soon after the murder of her father that the family was once more financially embarrassed. It seemed incredible but it was true. Gambling debts ran away with so much money. Creditors appeared. No more credit, they said, without payment of old debts. She ignored them, bent on pleasure; but they refused to be ignored and they took their cases to court.

The result of these actions was that a house at Nourar which belonged to the Marquis was ordered to be sold that the creditors might receive their just dues.

Marie, who evidently was fond of the house, was furious at the thought of losing it. Here again she shows her complete inability to understand the problems of others. She only saw as important what was so to herself; what happened to others was of no significance whatsoever. That is the murderer's outlook: seeing himself or herself all-important, the only—or almost the only—significant being in the world. And others (for example Sainte-Croix) are only significant in proportion to the pleasure they bring to the egoist.

She had been receiving the goods of certain tradesmen with never a thought of paying for them; her servants' wages had not been paid for months; that was of no account. But when a house was justly taken to pay her debts, she became wildly and senselessly furious.

She, who had had her lovers in the house, who cared nothing for her husband, had attempted to stab Mademoiselle Dufay. In the same mood, she retired to Nourar and attempted to set fire to the house there, rather than that it should fall into the hands of their creditors.

The attempt was not successful however. But, even though these creditors were satisfied, as she and her husband did not change their mode of life, it was not long before others were clamouring for payment of their dues.

So she began to look around for a further means of raising money.

*   *   *

The fortune her father left had been shared by herself, her two brothers and her sister, the Carmelite. If one of them died, his or her portion would be shared among the remaining members of the family.

To Sainte-Croix and Marie it seemed simple. Why should they not all die so that the entire fortune should be Marie's?

Sainte-Croix's ambition was clearly to become a professional poisoner, of the Exili class. He was continuing with his experiments in the Place Maubert, searching for the perfect poisons, those which killed without trace, and which could be regulated so as to produce a quick death or a lingering one. For such poisons he knew he would be paid high prices; and clients whom he had satisfied would be sure to treat him with the utmost respect at all times. Thus he saw before him a life of great power and riches through his work in the Place Maubert.

The murder of Marie's father was encouraging, although it had shown them, since the 'receipt' had to be administered so many times, that they were far from reaching perfection. He must find something which need be given only once. He must recapture the skill of the Borgias and the Medicis.

It seems to have been a good opportunity, from Sainte-Croix's point of view, to experiment on Marie's family while he was perfecting his art.

Marie's two brothers lived together. The elder, like his father, named Antoine, married about this time Marie Thérèse de Villarceau. She was a shrewd woman who had heard the stories of the scandalous life led by her sister-in-law and may, even at that time, have wondered whether there was not something a little suspicious in the way her father-in-law had died.

Her husband, Antoine, had, in addition to his portion of his father's wealth, inherited some of his father's offices. He already held the post of *Intendant* of Orléans and now became the Civil Lieutenant.

His brother was a *Conseiller au Parlement*. They were serious young men of wealth and position; and they enjoyed the confidences of the ministers.

The two conspirators realized that they must act with caution. Her brother's wife caused Marie some concern; the woman was sharp and already suspicious. It would not be wise, therefore, for Marie to feign friendship with the family and insinuate herself into the house, where she could slip the necessary poison into their food or drink. That would be out of the question.

No! The poison was not yet subtle enough to be safe. Therefore Sainte-Croix and Marie arranged that when her elder brother was travelling on the lonely road from Paris to Orléans, he should be set upon by cut-throats. Then his portion would be divided among the rest of the family.

Sainte-Croix agreed that this was a good idea, for it was very necessary that suspicion should not alight on the little room in the Place Maubert. Glaser was a nervous man; a little suspicion and he would be off, and without Glaser it would not be easy to carry on with his ambitions.

It was not difficult in those days to find desperate men who were ready to commit murder for a consideration; but the plan went wrong, for, at the last minute, Antoine met some friends who were travelling to Orléans, and they all decided to go together.

It was a very different matter for a couple of footpads to attack six men instead of one; and that plan failed.

Meanwhile Sainte-Croix and Marie had concocted a better plan.

Marie occasionally visited her brothers and sister-in-law, and as they were very conventional people they made a show of friendship towards her; and it was during one of these visits to her family that she heard how her younger brother's valet had left him suddenly, and that he was looking for another man to take that place.

Marie thought she saw here an excellent opportunity. She told her brothers that they needed a man of good character, someone who was recommended. She was not sure whether a certain man she had in mind was available, but would they wish her to make enquiries and find out?

They asked her to do so, and she hurried back to the Hôtel d'Aubray and at the first opportunity told Sainte-Croix what she had in mind.

His servant, La Chaussée, was, they both knew, a thoroughly loyal servant to them. He was also a man who needed money and was ready to do a great deal to get it. Why should they not in these circumstances make use of La Chaussée? He would make a perfect valet, and would be able to superintend the preparation of his master's food perhaps; or at least he would be able to interfere with it on its way from kitchen to table.

Sainte-Croix believed it could be done. It was to be a business deal between him and Marie. He would arrange this matter to her satisfaction, but he would need money, and La Chaussée would have to be paid for his part in the venture. Marie would understand that. She had no money, but she gave him two promissory notes, one for 25,000 the other for 30,000 livres.

When her share of her brother's fortune came her way, such sums would be of little account to her.

They probably wondered how they would manage to dispose of the Carmelite nun when her turn came, but they decided to take first things first, by performing the simplest murders; their experiences would enable them later to carry out the more difficult ones.

La Chaussée was groomed in his part and sent to the brothers who, finding him respectful, and thinking he would be efficient, engaged him.

La Chaussée's orders were, first to murder the elder brother; and this he set about doing with the utmost energy. He must have been too energetic, because Antoine d'Aubray, on drinking a glass of wine which had been brought to him by his valet, complained of its bitter taste.

No, Glaser's Receipt was far from perfect yet!

La Chaussée was a quick-witted rogue; it was this quality which had commended him to Sainte-Croix.

He looked astonished, took a spoon, sipped the wine and made a wry face. Then his expression lightened. He knew what it was. One of the servants had taken medicine that morning and had omitted to wash the glass! He would reprimand that servant. He greatly regretted that his master should have suffered this inconvenience through a servant's carelessness; it was preposterous. He took the wine, threw it into the fire with a dramatic gesture, carefully washed the glass and brought his master a glass of wine which had not been tampered with.

Antoine must have thought that La Chaussée was a good fellow. It was not his fault that his fellow-servants were careless, and when La Chaussée assured him that that sort of carelessness should not happen again, he was satisfied.

At Easter time it was necessary for the two brothers to go to their estate at Villequoy in Beauce. They did not intend to stay long so did not take many servants with them. But by this time La Chaussée had done his work so well that he had completely ingratiated himself with the pair of them. He was the perfect factotum, tactful, resourceful, always at hand when required. They were beginning to find that when he was not with them, they missed him. So to Villequoy went La Chaussée as the only personal servant to accompany the brothers.

So assiduously did he look after their comforts that he even ventured to the kitchen. One imagines his insistence: But *Monsieur le Lieutenant* likes his beef cooked this way! Or: *Monsieur le Conseiller* will have this dish well flavoured.

The outcome was that La Chaussée was often to be found in

the kitchen, and although it was not in the nature of his duty to be there, the kitchen staff tolerated him on account of the influence he had with their masters.

One day a giblet pie was made and La Chaussée had had a hand in its making. Antoine was particularly fond of giblet pie, and consequently ate a considerable amount of it.

It was noticed that all those who ate the pie were ill, and those who refused it were not. But the effect on Antoine was more terrible than on any of the others. It is possible that he was being slowly poisoned as his father had been.

He did not recover his health after eating the giblet pie, but grew worse; he lost his appetite and in a few days his weight had diminished so that he looked like a different man.

He said that he felt he had some malignant illness which had attacked him suddenly, and he must return to Paris at once to set his affairs in order.

La Chaussée was with him night and day, and Antoine was grateful. He told his brother that he did not know what they would do without La Chaussée; he was always at hand, anticipating every wish. When one was as ill as Antoine had become, one appreciated service like that.

His wife was horrified at the change in him. She shared the nursing with La Chaussée, and she too was grateful to the valet. But in spite of all her care—and because of La Chaussée's—Antoine died five days after his return to Paris.

Marie Thérèse, Antoine's wife, was too stricken with her grief to view the matter of his death with her usual shrewdness at that time; and at the autopsy, the doctor announced that Antoine d'Aubray d'Offémont had died of a 'malignant humour'.

*   *   *

The success of this venture made Marie and Sainte-Croix feel that they were invincible.

Two deaths in a short time; two autopsies; and yet the doctors had given verdicts of natural death. There must be no time wasted. The second brother must be given the same treatment.

Meanwhile Marie's children were growing up and she decided that they needed a tutor.

Her choice alighted on a young man who was a barrister and a Bachelor in Theology of the University of Paris. His name was Jean Briancourt; he was handsome but needy, and he looked upon it as great good fortune to be given a chance to serve such families as the Gobelins and the d'Aubrays.

He arrived full of hope, not realizing that he was entering one of the most sinister households in France.

The family consisted of five children (three boys and two girls), and when he had made their acquaintance he felt that he could work adequately with them. But it was when he met Madame de Brinvilliers that he must have begun to wonder whether he had been so wise in coming to this house.

Marie was one of those women who have no doubt whatsoever of their own attractiveness. She would throw herself into a circle of men and, before they had time to escape, look about as though to say: See how the men surround me and how I find it difficult to escape from them! The tutor was unworldly and ready to accept her own valuation of herself. But Briancourt was a man with a conscience; he wanted to be virtuous, but he was possessed of the same desires as most young men, and no sooner had he set eyes on the woman whose little body seemed to contain such energy and determination, whose blue eyes sparkled with invitation and whose sensuality was apparent even to such as he was, than he realized that temptation was at hand.

What he did not realize was that she deliberately intended to tempt him; and that the reason was not because of admiration for his youth or his charm, but because she wished to subjugate her servants and use them as she and Sainte-Croix had used La Chaussée.

He began to think it was fortunate that he had come only for the holidays and that, when they were over, he was to leave the household and continue his studies at the Sorbonne.

He joined the family in Marie's country house at Sains in Picardy, and during the first weeks Marie showed her great interest in him. She made no pretence of interest in her children. It was clear to many that one of the girls—the plain one—irritated her beyond measure, and the poor little creature made herself scarce whenever her mother was in the house.

A strange thing happened to Briancourt during those first weeks. He was warned to leave the house. In the weeks to come he must deeply have regretted that he had not taken that advice.

One of the pages, who was Marie's husband's servant rather than hers, asked Briancourt to walk away from the house with him one evening that they might not be overheard, and when the tutor did so, told him many startling stories about the Marquise de Brinvilliers.

The servants saw, he said, that Madame had turned her eyes on the tutor, and therefore Monsieur Briancourt would

do well to tread warily. He told of their mistress's liaison with
Sainte-Croix which had resulted in the latter's incarceration in
the Bastille. Madame had had other lovers . . . many of them.
The tutor should take care that he would not be counted
among them. If an important gentleman like Monsieur de
Sainte-Croix could be sent to the Bastille, what could happen
to a humble tutor?

Briancourt may have decided to avoid his mistress; he may
have congratulated himself that as soon as the vacation was
over he would be hard at work at the Sorbonne. All he had to
do was keep away from this alarming yet fascinating woman.

He had yet to learn that Marie—not himself—would be the
one to decide on the nature of their relationship.

*   *   *

It seemed to Marie and Sainte-Croix that, as they had been
so successful with her father and brother and the doctors had
not discovered their deaths had been due to poison, it was
foolish to delay further. They sent orders to La Chaussée to
proceed at once with his second murder.

La Chaussée went to work with a will. He was highly
thought of by the Conseiller, who wanted no one else to look
after him but his faithful La Chaussée. So La Chaussée
nursed him as carefully as he had nursed Antoine d'Aubray,
sitting up with him through the night and preparing his food.

"You are a good servant," the Conseiller told La Chaussée.
"I am going to leave you a hundred *écus* in my will to show my
appreciation."

La Chaussée received the news with gratitude, but naturally
it did not make such a rogue wish to prolong his master's life;
and the same illness as that which had attacked his brother
took hold of the poor gentleman—only in his case it seemed
even more malignant, more violent.

It was soon understood that he could not live, and a message
was sent to Marie in Sains that she must come to Paris immediately if she wished to see her brother alive.

*   *   *

The Aubray estate would now be divided between Marie,
her Carmelite sister, and the widow of her brother. Marie
should be financially secure, but naturally she did not propose
to share the estate with anyone. She must discuss plans for the
removal of the two women as quickly as was possible.

But in the meantime, Madame d'Aubray—her brother
Antoine's widow—showed signs of being difficult.

She was thinking what a strange thing it was that her father-in-law should die, then her husband, immediately followed by her brother-in-law—and all within a short space of time. Throughout the whole country there was a great deal of talk about poison, and she was suspicious.

Sainte-Croix and Marie waited uneasily for the autopsy. The doctors were not so glib this time. They too thought that three deaths in one family were matters for close consideration.

They studied the state of the internal organs of the dead man; they drew up their report. Doctors of today would say that there was no doubt, from their findings, that death had been due to poison. In those days doctors naturally lacked much of the knowledge which is commonplace today; and those who examined the dead man's body, while they suspected poison, were unsure. It may have been that, knowing those who would profit from this man's death were influential people, they had no wish to take the responsibility of accusing them of murder.

Accordingly at the autopsy there was no mention of poison; and once again it seemed to Sainte-Croix and Marie that they had been successful.

Their thoughts immediately turned to the removal of those others who stood between Marie and full possession of her father's fortune.

*   *   *

When Marie returned to Sains, she renewed her attentions to the tutor.

At that time she must have behaved like a woman intoxicated with success. She became careless, certain of her own powers; even more than before she saw herself as the only significant person in the world.

She made Briancourt sit with her in the evenings, and their talk was of poison—a subject which fascinated her. The tutor confessed that he knew very little about poisons, but he did know that it was the Italians who excelled in this dubious art. He talked to her of what he had read concerning the Borgias and the Medicis. She listened avidly; and to her the talk of poisonings must have been more exhilarating than lovers' whisperings between them.

Marie told him that she had heard of a woman who had grown rich through the use of poison; she had been so clever, so subtle, that no one guessed what she was doing. It was so easy. One just removed all those whose deaths would bring profit. The woman who had done this was brilliantly clever; he must admit that.

According to evidence which he gave later, Briancourt replied that he did not believe that the woman, although she may have achieved wealth, had gained happiness. Madame de Brinvilliers laughed at such naïvety, but her laughter had a caressing quality. Why, she explained, at the end of her life that woman could go into a convent and repent; that would secure her place in Heaven. She was clearly a clever woman, determined to have the best of both worlds; for what good was wealth to an old woman? And to a young one the immediate pleasure which Earth had to offer must be preferable to the glory of the life to come.

Conversations of this sort were far from comforting to a young man such as Briancourt.

*　　　*　　　*

Marie looked at her plain daughter and thought the girl tiresome.

What hope was there for her in the world? She would need a handsome *dot* if she were to attract a husband; and then he would never be faithful; not that that was of any great importance; but how would such an oddity find lovers to console her?

Marie gave the girl a dose of Glaser's Receipt, but almost immediately afterwards she regretted this. She had been over-exuberant, over-anxious to make use of the fascinating stuff on another victim. That was folly. Victims should be chosen with care.

The poor child was then ordered to drink lots of milk— the best antidote for arsenic—and in a short time recovered; but often Marie was tempted to dose her again, and indeed did so. But the milk cure always followed.

She must have felt annoyed with herself for wasting time on the girl when there were two others who still stood in the way of her enjoyment of the whole of her father's fortune.

*　　　*　　　*

When Briancourt went with the family to Paris he made the acquaintance of Sainte-Croix, who visited the Hôtel d'Aubray frequently. He often brought with him a man named Colbeau who was introduced as one of his closest friends.

The Marquis de Brinvilliers had remained at Sains; at this time he seemed to have a preference for the country.

Marie was in debt again, and some of her creditors had even seized her coach as their due; Marie was furious at this on the grounds that it was useless against the mounting debts. It may have been that the reason the Marquis stayed in the country was to escape *his* creditors, since the life of Paris was as much to his taste, as it was to Marie's.

Sainte-Croix and his friend Colbeau advised Marie that, if bribes were offered in the right quarters, even though her creditors took her to court, it would avail them nothing. Briancourt, whom Marie was petting so much that she had begun to treat him as a trusted friend and adviser, heard this suggestion and was shocked by it. As soon as he was alone with her he told her that she would be very misguided if she took the advice of men such as Sainte-Croix and Colbeau who were clearly rogues.

Marie must have smiled inwardly at the naïvety of the tutor, and she probably decided that she must prepare him quickly for the part he had to play.

When they left Paris once more for Sains, their first stop on the road was at Louvres-en-Parisis where they stayed the night at an inn named *Le Grand Cerf*.

There she talked to him very confidentially and, as she must have planned to do, seduced him. During that night she told him about the poisonings, and how Sainte-Croix had supplied the 'Receipt'. She explained how La Chaussée had been insinuated into the household and had doctored the food.

Briancourt was stunned. Moreover he must have been in a quandary because he believed himself to be in love with Marie and did not know what to make of this strange confession. She even explained to him that the poison was in the form of liquid and powder and contained *venin de crapaud*.

Briancourt said later, when giving his evidence, that he implored her to have no more to do with Sainte-Croix, who was her evil genius; he implored her to repent and make amends for her wicked deeds. She laughed at him affection-ately, and the poor young man must have felt that he had entered a mad world, for she seemed to take this terrible act of murder by poison so calmly.

This normal man, as yet inexperienced of the world, had found himself face to face with a murderess, who, for her own reasons, had decided to be perfectly frank with him. It must have been very difficult for a man such as Briancourt to understand this woman.

But he was young and she was beautiful—more than that, she was sexually knowledgeable; she may have seemed like a messenger from the devil, but he could not resist her.

He had become her lover and her confidant, all in a short

night; he was very young, and these two facts must have completely bewildered him.

They arrived at the *château* at Sains where the Marquis de Brinvilliers was staying with the younger children. It was a fantastic household, and it is not surprising that Briancourt grew more and more apprehensive.

He must have wondered why he had been told these secrets. He knew that Marie watched him closely, and he began to ask himself whether she regretted taking him into her confidence. It occurred to him that he ought to watch very carefully what food he ate, for he knew she had a casket in which she kept packets which had come from the Place Maubert. He no doubt felt at times that he was living in a nightmare.

Marie was certainly unsure of him. She must have sent a message to Sainte-Croix telling him of her fears concerning the tutor, for very soon after they arrived at the *château*, Sainte-Croix paid a visit.

The tutor looked on at this amazing household. He had already learned that Sainte-Croix had been Marie's lover, and for that her father had had him imprisoned in the Bastille; but Monsieur de Brinvilliers seemed to have no objection to his visiting the *château*. In fact he seemed delighted to have him there, for there can be no doubt that Sainte-Croix was a witty and amusing companion who would enliven country life considerably for the Marquis, who was forced to stay away from the town. Briancourt had heard that before Sainte-Croix became so closely associated with Madame he had been the great friend of her husband.

They all walked in the gardens of the *château* together and Marie insisted that Briancourt join them. She made no secret of her fondness for the tutor, and this embarrassed him; but no one else seemed to mind in the least.

*   *   *

Having Sainte-Croix at the *château*, and seeing him, in all the glory of his wit and charm, in contrast with her rake of a husband and the shy young tutor, Marie thought how much she would prefer to be married to the Gascon adventurer. And why should anything she desired be denied her? Of course she had a husband and Sainte-Croix had a wife; but for what purpose were the experiments in the Place Maubert conducted, if not to remove obstacles such as these?

It was so simple to give the Marquis a little dose. He was ill immediately, and he might have died had not Sainte-Croix— who seemed able to read Marie's thoughts—followed the dose with his own specially effective antidote. The Marquis made a miraculous recovery. Sainte-Croix was now on the alert; so was the Marquis.

Sainte-Croix certainly had no wish to marry Marie; he would never feel safe if he did. Therefore he was determined to keep her married to the Marquis and to stay married himself to the quiet little wife who gave him no trouble. He must be very careful, always ready with the antidote should he see any signs of poison having been given to his friend. He must have warned the Marquis of what might happen to him, for he— Sainte-Croix—had no intention of staying long in the country. Moreover, Briancourt noticed that the Marquis became very careful about what he ate and drank. He did not sit at the table but close to the buffet where he could watch the food and drink. He would only allow his personal valet to serve him. Once or twice he remarked: "Don't change my glass, and wash it every time you give me something to drink."

Yet, in spite of this atmosphere of suspicion, there was much gaiety at the *château*, and the Marquis seemed to bear his wife no ill will.

*   *   *

One night when Briancourt went to bed he could not sleep. He must have been terrified of this strange household.

He was asked later why he did not leave at this stage. He was an impecunious young man and the times, for such as he, were hard. It was not easy to find employment and he had been sent to the Brinvilliers family on recommendation from a lawyer, Monsieur Bocager, which he had believed to be a wonderful piece of good luck. To walk out of such a cherished post would have deeply offended Monsieur Bocager who had friends in high places. It would certainly not have been easy to find another post. But perhaps most important of all, he was completely fascinated by Marie.

On this particular night, while he was trying to sleep, Marie rushed into his room. She shut the door and looked at him wildly. "Take care!" she cried. "You have wormed secrets of the greatest confidence out of me. Therefore you would be wise to take care."

Briancourt leaped out of bed, and implored her to calm herself. She made him swear that he would never repeat what she had told him about the murders, and he assured her that he never would. Then he asked her if she would release him from his duties as his great desire was to get back to Paris.

She told him tenderly that she did not wish him to go, and

said that he had nothing to fear if only he would be discreet;
and if he were so she would make his fortune, so that he need
not worry any more about having to tutor the children of the
rich.

He wanted to protest, but she stopped his protests with
kisses.

She asked him to excuse her for a moment and she disappeared; a few minutes later she returned with Sainte-Croix,
who remained in the bedroom to the bewilderment of the
astonished young man while they talked together of what good
friends they all were.

Briancourt began to realize that the object of this strange
scene was to show him that he was now one of them; he shared
their guilty secrets and if he betrayed them it might be difficult
for him to prove that he was without guilt.

Sainte-Croix announced the following morning that business
matters in Paris called him, and asked the tutor to ride with
him a little distance to put him on the right road. This Briancourt did, and, as they rode together, Sainte-Croix attempted
to entertain him with lewd stories of his exploits. He had
decided that the young man must be demoralized as quickly as
possible. Sainte-Croix and Marie were not only irritated, but
made anxious by those who showed signs of possessing con-
sciences.

*   *   *

When Briancourt left Sainte-Croix and returned to the
château, Marie—as must have been agreed between her and
Sainte-Croix—told him what would be required of him.

In this affair the next victim was to be Marie's sister, the
Carmelite. It was with regard to her that they decided to make
use of the tutor. The family was becoming suspicious of Marie,
and she could not therefore introduce any new servants into her
sister's household. It was for this reason that Briancourt was to
ingratiate himself with her, and as he was a Bachelor in
Theology, he should find this an easy matter. When he had won
her confidence he must turn her against her gardener—it
should not be difficult to trump up some charge against the
man, insisted Marie, for her pious sister was very ready to see
the faults of others—and introduce a new one to her. The
new one would be La Chaussée who had already worked
effectively.

Briancourt was horrified. Marie used all her powers of
persuasion. She was really concerned for her children's inherit-
ance, she told the tutor. Her sister was planning to leave a vast

proportion of her fortune to a lady who was her great friend and
who had turned devout now that she was growing old. The
lady had been the mistress of Gaston of Orléans who was
brother to Louis XIII. Could Marie look on and see her
children lose what was theirs by right?

But Briancourt would not be impressed by such talk. He
was asked to assist at the murder of a woman—a woman who
was known for her piety. He could not hide his disgust and
Marie was perturbed.

She made light of his reluctance but there would have been
a glitter in her eyes. She did not trust him; if she were not
careful, instead of being a help he would be a menace.

Briancourt was aware of her displeasure and from now on he
knew that he would have to keep a closer watch on what he ate
and drank.

It became necessary for the eldest Brinvilliers boy to go to
Paris, and thither he went, the tutor and Marie accompanying
him.

Briancourt guessed that Sainte-Croix would have been told
of his unwillingness to co-operate, and he was desperately
afraid, while he was still undecided what to do.

Could he go to the authorities and tell them that the woman,
who had been and still was his mistress, was planning to poison
her sister? It seemed to him a terrible position for a young man
to find himself in. He was distraught.

Sainte-Croix now thought that it would be wiser not to use
La Chaussée for the murder of Mademoiselle d'Aubray. It
seemed hardly likely that a gardener would be able to worm
his way into the house to the required extent. There was, on
the other hand, Colbeau's daughter. She was a clever girl and
had already formed an acquaintance with Mademoiselle
d'Aubray, feigning a desire to enter a convent and asking the
old lady's advice about this.

This young girl was willing to undertake the task of poisoning
Mademoiselle d'Aubray; but the price she asked was the high
one of one thousand pistoles.

Marie and Sainte-Croix agreed that this price was exorbi-
tant, so there was no immediate action. In fact their thoughts
had turned to the widow, Madame d'Aubray, who was also on
the list.

La Chaussée, to show how willingly he was prepared to
work, had already been to see her, and was trying to persuade
her to take him back into her service.

Accordingly, interest was switched from Marie's sister to her
sister-in-law.

Briancourt was horrified and begged Marie to stop and
consider what fresh sins she was adding to those already committed. He earnestly declared that he would never be induced
to take any part in such horrible schemes.

*   *   *

Briancourt had now become a dangerous man, and Sainte-
Croix and Marie decided that there was only one course left
to them. Sainte-Croix brought two of his servants to the hôtel,
for he was staying there often now and appeared to have made
it his home while the Marquis stayed in the country. The
servants were La Chaussée and a man named Bazile.

Briancourt knew enough of their methods to guess that their
plan was now to poison *him*. Very carefully he watched, and
he actually discovered the man Bazile in the act of putting
something into the goblet from which he, Briancourt, was about
to drink.

Briancourt thrashed the man soundly; then he went to
Marie, looked at her sternly, told her what he had discovered,
and demanded that the man be immediately dismissed.

Marie pretended to be shocked, and Bazile was dismissed.

*   *   *

Marie's attempts to murder seem very clumsy, and it appears
that her very arrogance made her so careless.

As soon as Bazile was dismissed she bought a beautiful
tapestry bed, called the tutor to her room to admire it and then
suggested that they would find great pleasure in sharing it.

She demanded that he come to her bedroom at midnight for
the assignation; but living in this household of intrigue had
made Briancourt suspicious.

At the hôtel in the Rue Neuve Saint-Paul there was a gallery
which overlooked the windows of the bedroom which was used
by the Marquise, and, feeling that the affair of the tapestry bed
was a strange one, as it began to get dark Briancourt went into
this gallery in order that he might watch through the windows
and discover what preparations were being made in the bedroom.

Eventually he saw Marie enter the room and light the candles. Fortunately for Briancourt she did not draw the curtains
and he could see clearly what was taking place in the room.
She went to the chimney piece which, after the fashion of the
day, was enormous and fitted with two shutters used when there
was no fire as, being so large a fireplace, there was apt to be a
strong draught when the wind was high. These shutters were

closed and bolted when there was no fire in the room, and
Briancourt watched Marie unbolt them.

Sainte-Croix, disguised as an artisan, stepped from the
chimney place into the room.

He and Marie sat down at a table and began talking earnestly, making plans which, in view of what he knew of these
two, Briancourt guessed concerned what they planned to do to
himself when he was asleep. Then Sainte-Croix went back to
his hiding place and the shutters were closed.

Briancourt did not know what to do. He was not afraid of
physical violence, for he was young and strong; but he was
horrified beyond measure at the depths to which Marie was
prepared to go, and that she could invite him to her room to be
her lover when her real motive was to lure him to what might
well be his death.

At midnight he went to her bedroom. She tried to be
seductive, but he was not to be deceived. He demanded suddenly how she could be so wantonly cruel. What had he done,
he asked, that she should want to have him assassinated?

Sainte-Croix, who had been listening, realized that their
plot to take the young man by surprise had been discovered;
he came out of his hiding place, the artisan's hat pulled down
over his face and making a good disguise. But when he had
looked through the window from the gallery, Briancourt had
seen Sainte-Croix without his hat, so there was no question of
the latter's hiding his identity. Briancourt immediately began
to reproach Sainte-Croix, calling him by his name.

It was quite a different matter, killing a sleeping man, from
tackling him when he was awake—particularly if he were
lithe and strong as Briancourt was—and Sainte-Croix decided
that the best thing he could do was get away as quickly as
possible. He ran to the door and escaped by way of the stair-
case.

Briancourt made no attempt to follow him. He turned to
Marie and solemnly accused her of trying to bring about his
death, first by poisoning, then by assassination.

She became hysterical and denied having any part in the
plots.

He knew this was false and told her so, but she retaliated
by telling him that if he did not believe her, she would poison
herself.

She had always talked glibly of poisons, so that he believed
she might do this in her present hysterical condition; and when
she went to her casket of poisons, took out something and
made the motion of slipping it into her mouth, Briancourt

was afraid she might have meant what she said. He managed
to wrest it from her and made her promise not to do anything
so wicked.

After she had wept and stormed and implored him to believe
her, Briancourt said that he would overlook what she had tried
to do to him, if she would promise not to kill herself and would
agree that he might leave the house.

She promised then that she would not take poison; he made
her lie down, but she insisted that he sit by her bed, which—he
said in his evidence—he did all through the night.

*   *   *

Sainte-Croix did not confine his activities to the poisoning
of the Brinvilliers family. His scheme had been to sell his
poisons—his secret, subtle poisons—and grow rich; and as a
result of his discoveries and the business deals he had arranged,
there was an outbreak of sudden death throughout France.

One man who had become a friend of Sainte-Croix was a
certain Pierre Louis de Reich de Pennautier, a very ambitious
man, who had come a long way; although he had begun life as
a clerk he had lost no time in climbing from success to success.

He began by marrying a wealthy heiress, and that was the
beginning of his good fortune, for his father-in-law, Monsieur
Lesecq, died young and, since he had been the Treasurer to
the States of Languedoc, Pennautier took over the office.

There was, however, a certain amount of suspicion attached
to Lesecq's death, and his widow would no longer receive
Pennautier, whose wife also left him. Pennautier, however, was
not perturbed. He was only concerned in getting what he
wanted from life, and he had had what he set out to get from
the Lesecqs.

He prospered and grew very rich, but his riches only made
him more ambitious. Pennautier longed to add not only to his
revenues but to his power; and he had his greedy eyes on the
Receivership-General of the Clergy of France. This office was
worth a considerable annual income—60,000 livres.

Mennevillette, the man who held this coveted position, had
a chief assistant named Saint-Laurent; and it became clear
that on the resignation of Mennevillette, the post would go to
his chief assistant.

There was very little hope of Pennautier's being elected,
and as Saint-Laurent was by no means an old man, it was no
use waiting hopefully for his retirement. Pennautier then
began to use all his influence, which was great, to prevent
Saint-Laurent's succeeding to the post. He suggested—when

he realized that Saint-Laurent would certainly be elected—that they should share it as it was a great deal for one man to do alone, but Saint-Laurent indignantly refused the offer. Pennautier then made attempts to persuade the clergy that Saint-Laurent was unfitted for the job.

So energetic was Pennautier, and so great his influence, that he succeeded, and Saint-Laurent was forced to retire from the contest. But, Mennevillette, the original Receiver-General with whom Saint-Laurent had been working for so many years, was determined that his protégé, and not Pennautier, should succeed to the title; and he therefore declared that, as there was so much controversy, he would come out of his retirement and take up his old duties.

He did so, named Saint-Laurent as his successor and then resigned. Those who had watched the battle now declared that there was only one course open to Pennautier; he must retire gracefully.

But there came into the household of Saint-Laurent at that time a young man named George; he was valet to the Receiver-General and he had been recommended by Sainte-Croix.

Almost immediately Saint-Laurent was taken violently ill and died. Madame Saint-Laurent was certain that he had been poisoned and insisted on an autopsy, but before this had taken place the valet, George, took fright and disappeared.

The autopsy did not indicate poison, and as the Receiver-General had fallen from his horse some short time before his death, the doctors said that this fall had contributed largely to his end.

But Madame de Saint-Laurent was dissatisfied with the verdict; the constant talk of poison, the rumours which were ever present, and the mysterious disappearance of the valet had made her very uneasy and she did not hesitate to make her fears known. She demanded that a search be made for George.

The valet was seen in the streets one day by a priest who knew the Saint-Laurent family well. He called to George, shouting that the family were very eager to see him; but, realizing that he was recognized, George responded by taking to his heels and running as if for his life. Madame de Saint-Laurent complained to the authorities, but George was not found.

Pennautier then stepped into the post which he had coveted; there was more work for him to do and he took a partner named d'Alibert. It may have been that d'Alibert brought money into his business and that Pennautier, dealing with Sainte-Croix (and it is presumed that he was dealing with Sainte-Croix) needed money.

D'Alibert died suddenly, and his wife demanded to see the accounts of that business in which her husband had a share; but Pennautier was determined that she should not do this. He was not the slightest bit alarmed by the scenes which his partner's widow was threatening to make; but it appeared that she had a brother, a Monsieur de la Magdelène who, being a man of affairs, approached Pennautier on behalf of the widow, declaring that he was determined to see that his sister had her rights.

Monsieur de la Magdelène died suddenly and in exactly the way in which Monsieur d'Alibert had died. The deaths were said to be due to apoplexy.

Madame d'Alibert had now lost her only friend and adviser, and she had no idea how to proceed against such a wily financier as Pennautier; she was reduced to complete poverty.

Now Pennautier was almost at the top. The Minister Colbert became his friend. He was one of the wealthiest men in France and fast becoming one of the most influential.

But such a man was certain to arouse envy; and rumours concerning the manner in which Pennautier had achieved his success were circulating in Paris.

Sainte-Croix heard these rumours; and as certain people who greatly envied Pennautier had accused the latter of crimes such as coining false money, and so insistent had been these accusations that, in spite of Pennautier's position, police had searched his house, the Gascon began to wonder what might happen if the rumours concerning the numerous deaths, which had occurred so conveniently, were investigated.

Pennautier was a clever man; there was no doubt that he himself would emerge safely; but what of his friends?

Sainte-Croix thought it might not be a bad idea if he too held a position of influence in the country. He had heard that there was a vacant post in the King's household. Sainte-Croix longed for this; but like all places at Court, this one had to be bought, and its price was 100,000 ecus.

Sainte-Croix did not possess the money, but Pennautier was a rich man; and Sainte-Croix was surely in a position to ask Pennautier to provide it.

He decided to approach the great man cautiously, but in a manner which would allow him to make no mistake as to his, Sainte-Croix's, intentions.

*   *   *

Sainte-Croix died suddenly in his laboratory.

Madame de Sainte-Croix, wondering why he had remained there so long, went into the laboratory to see what had become of him, and discovered him lying on the floor near the stove. The glass mask which he used when working on his dangerous brews was, so it is said, lying broken beside him on the floor.

The cause of Sainte-Croix's death is not known, but there have been many interesting theories put forward.

Dumas Père, who was fascinated by the story, wrote that Sainte-Croix had been trying to make poisons such as had been used by the Medicis, and was, at the time of his death, endeavouring to produce one, the fumes of which would kill, without the victim's taking it in food or drink. He was looking, says Dumas, for a poison such as that which, it was rumoured, had been used on the poisoned gloves which had killed Jeanne of Navarre, or that which was smeared on flowers, so that those smelling them would immediately expire.

He goes on to suggest that Sainte-Croix was brewing some such concoction when the mask broke and he inhaled the fatal poison.

I have read one purely imaginary version of the manner of Sainte-Croix's dying, in a work of fiction, and in this the author suggests that one of his numerous enemies, knowing in what he was engaged, broke the strings of the mask while he was in Sainte-Croix's company and fixed it with some resinous compound, so that when Sainte-Croix bent over the evaporating dish on the furnace, the resinous substance melted, the mask fell to the floor and Sainte-Croix inhaled the deadly poison.

Some authorities state that Sainte-Croix had been ill for several months and that he had some sort of fit whilst working in his laboratory.

Was Sainte-Croix, who had committed so many murders, himself murdered? He was at the time attempting to blackmail Pennautier who was as callous a murderer as he was himself; his relations with Marie had deteriorated considerably, and it is said that he had tried to poison her and would have done so if she, recognizing immediately the symptoms of arsenical poisoning, had not known exactly how to counteract the poison.

If Marie or Pennautier had killed Sainte-Croix they would surely not have left in his possession certain documents which could incriminate them.

It may be—and perhaps this is the most likely solution— that Sainte-Croix was one of the few people, concerned in this long line of eliminations, who died from natural causes.

His death was the beginning of disaster for his colleagues.

When they heard of it, and that his laboratory had been searched, both Pennautier and Marie knew that they were in grave danger.

*   *   *

Marie was at her country estate of Picpus at the time.
Pennautier, who knew that Marie was as deeply involved with
Sainte-Croix as he was himself, sent a letter to her there,
advising her of what had happened. Marie hastened to Paris
as soon as she received the letter.

It may have been that Madame de Sainte-Croix had been
jealous of Marie; it may have been that she directed the
attention of the authorities to a red casket about which, she
informed them, her husband had always been deeply concerned,
telling them that he had said that, in the event of his death, the
casket was to be given to the Marquise de Brinvilliers, and that
there was a packet inside which was for Monsieur de Pennautier.

When this became known both Marie and Pennautier made
great efforts to get possession of the casket and offered bribes
right and left to everybody who they thought could help to
bring it into their hands.

But the casket was opened by the police, and in it were
found documents to indicate that sums of money had been paid
to Sainte-Croix by Marie and Pennautier. The packets in the
casket were found to contain various poisons: arsenic, vitriol,
antimony. There were documents which showed that Marie
had promised to pay Sainte-Croix certain sums; there was a
packet of letters from her to Sainte-Croix which left no doubt
of the relationship which had once existed between them.
There were references to Glaser's Receipt. Other powders
were discovered, together with a bottle of what appeared to be
pure water. This was analysed and no poison could be found in
it; but when it was administered to animals they immediately
died, though no trace of poison could be found in their organs.
It seemed that Sainte-Croix had come very close to rediscover-
ing the secrets of the Borgias and the Medicis.

Two widows came forward. One was the widow of Saint-
Laurent, who accused Pennautier of poisoning her husband
with the help of Sainte-Croix; the other was Madame d'Aubray,
the widow of Marie's elder brother.

The police went to Picpus to arrest Marie, after she had
hastily left Paris. But she was already on her way to England.

*   *   *

Pennautier was questioned. He was a man of great influence
and power, and had many friends at Court.

It was remembered that three years earlier Madame
Henriette d'Angleterre, the wife of the King's brother, had died
suddenly, and that many people had believed her death to have
been brought about by poison.

There was one, it was said, who might have had a hand in the murder of Madame, if murdered she had been, and that was Monsieur himself, for he and his wife had been on very bad terms.

Monsieur d'Orléans was the brother of the King of France, and Madame was the sister of the King of England. Charles II had loved his sister dearly, and the relationship between Charles of England and Louis of France had been strained by the death of Madame; and, although the autopsy declared her to have died from natural causes, Charles had not been entirely satisfied.

That had happened three years before, but the King of England still thought of his sister frequently and mourned her as sadly as one of his resilient nature could be expected to mourn anyone.

The rumours indicated that if this enquiry persisted there would be others involved besides Pennautier and the Marquise de Brinvilliers. It would be interesting to see what secrets were uncovered. But there were many who were determined that these secrets should never be uncovered.

Madame de Brinvilliers had gone to England knowing that the King of that country was notoriously lenient, and also that, having his own laboratory, he was very interested in the experiments made by other people. Even so, in view of the scandals which this case had set in motion, Louis felt he must bring back one of the suspected people to face a trial. He may have thought that it would be safer to let Madame de Brinvilliers stand trial than to let Pennautier. So he asked the King of England to send his subject back to France.

Charles was lazy. He could not offend Louis, of course; but it did go against his nature to send a woman to a harsh punishment, particularly if she were a pretty one.

He assured Louis that his will should be regarded as law in England, but he delayed so long in the matter that Marie had time to leave the country and find refuge in Holland. As the relationship between Holland and France was not a friendly one, it was no simple matter to persuade the Dutch to deport her.

So, with Madame de Brinvilliers in hiding, and Monsieur de Pennautier's being too dangerous and too influential a man to have his affairs probed into, the matter was officially allowed to drop.

But the police agent, Desgrez, was determined that one day he would bring the poisoners to justice.

*   *   *

When he heard that Sainte-Croix was dead, La Chaussée immediately disappeared. Madame d'Aubray, who was determined that Marie should be brought to justice, then realized that the valet must have had some connection with Sainte-Croix, and she remembered that Marie had introduced the man to her household. She was determined that La Chaussée should be found and questioned.

One of Madame d'Aubray's maids was being courted by a sergeant of the police named Cluet, and this girl was able to give him a great deal of information. La Chaussée had lodged with a barber in the Rue de Grenelle whilst he was working for the d'Aubrays, and had boasted to the barber that his employment with the d'Aubrays was in truth a blind; he was no valet; he was far more important; there was someone behind the scenes for whom he worked. Cluet visited the barber's shop often and during the course of gossip learned a good deal about La Chaussée.

One day La Chaussée was picked up in the streets of Paris. He was questioned; he was told that poisons had been found in the room over the barber's shop. He protested that they were remedies for skin diseases and that he had never administered poison to anyone; but later, when torture was applied, he confessed, and explained that he had been introduced into the household of the d'Aubrays and had poisoned both brothers while valeting them. He betrayed that he had been paid to do this by Sainte-Croix and the Marquise de Brinvilliers.

Eventually he was taken to the Place de Grève where his body was broken on the wheel.

*   *   *

Marie lived for three years in Holland where she was very poor and would have starved but for her sister, the nun whom she had planned to poison and who had only survived because Sainte-Croix had died when he did. This sister discovered where Marie was and sent her money regularly.

Marie was therefore able to live very quietly with one servant, and indeed she would have had no wish to live other than quietly for, during those three years, she must have been continually on the watch for someone who would recognize her and carry news to France of her hiding place.

She lived in Cambrai, Valenciennes and Antwerp; and finally she went to Liège where she boarded in a convent.

It was while she was in this convent that she wrote the confession in which she admitted that she had poisoned her father and had had her two brothers poisoned; she admitted that she had planned to poison her sister, and that she had given poison both to her husband and to her daughter.

Why did Marie write such a confession?

I do not think it was due to the religious influence of the convent. I think she was glorying in her crimes, that, living as she was, in such humble retirement, she had need to remind herself how powerful she had once been, how she had cleverly wiped from her path any who threatened her comfort. Arrogance is one of the chief characteristics of such murderers.

But deeply she was to regret having written that confession.

She had her enemies, but there were two who had made up their minds that they would bring her to justice. These were the women whose husbands she had poisoned, and they were determined not to rest until she received her just punishment for the misery she had brought into their lives. One was Madame de Saint-Laurent; the other was her sister-in-law, Madame d'Aubray.

They spared no effort in tracing her, and they discovered that she had settled in Liège.

There was one other who was eager to bring her to justice: Desgrez.

On discovering that she was living in the convent—which Madame d'Aubray may have done through her sister-in-law, the Carmelite—the two women may have approached Desgrez. I think this is very probably how it happened, because Desgrez —who would otherwise have known very little about Marie except that she was a ruthless poisoner—made exactly the right approach; and I feel that he must have been coached in this by the two women who would know of Marie's vanity where the opposite sex was concerned.

Disguised as a French abbé, young, handsome and so gallant—he was about thirty-six and near Marie's own age— Desgrez arrived in Liège.

He paid court to Marie, visiting her at the convent. She was flattered and, believing herself to be as attractive as ever, thought that his visits were entirely due to her charm.

The convent was a sanctuary and Desgrez could not arrest her while she was there, but at length he persuaded her to leave its sheltering walls and take a walk with him; the scenery along the Ourthe was very beautiful, he told her ardently, and he longed to show it to her.

One imagines Marie's eyes sparkling at the thought of a new love affair. After her long retirement and her quiet life it must have been very pleasant to feel herself admired once more. The temptation was naturally irresistible. She set out for

the walk with Desgrez and, as they sauntered along by the
river and he paid her the compliments which she knew so well
as the preliminaries to seduction, a coach trundled towards
them. Marie could not have noticed it at first, so engrossed
would she have been in the man she believed to be her admirer.
But Desgrez would be on the alert as the coach drew up beside
them and police officers stepped out.

Although Liège was neutral territory, the French were in
occupation and, strangely enough, were due to evacuate the
town that very day. Desgrez must have had some uneasy
moments for, if he had been unable to persuade Marie to
accompany him while Liège was still under French rule, he
would have found it very difficult to make the arrest.

The good luck, which had attended Marie all through her
criminal career, suddenly deserted her. If she had not gone for
that walk with Desgrez at that time she might never have been
brought to justice.

She was forced to get into the coach, and one imagines the
intensity of her rage when she realized that her 'admirer' was,
in fact, her betrayer.

She was frantic, especially when she learned that her confession, which she had written somewhat lightheartedly, was in
the hands of Desgrez.

She tried to commit suicide by breaking her glass during a
meal and swallowing the pieces, but Desgrez was on the
watch. He had made up his mind that she should not evade her
trial and punishment.

She was closely guarded during the journey from Liège to
Paris; and she must have hated Desgrez as she had hated few
others.

*   *   *

On the 17th April, 1676, Marie was examined at Mézières.
She was by this time calm and cool, and so sure of her super-
iority over her judges, that her courage returned.

She would outwit all as she had from the beginning of her
wicked career. She denied everything of which she was accused.

But Desgrez brought her to Paris, and she was taken to a cell
in the Conciergerie.

*   *   *

It was inevitable, during the examination of Marie, that the
name of Pennautier should arise; and since a lady of the
nobility was held in custody, there was no reason why a
financier should not be.

Pennautier was arrested.

The servants of Marie's house were questioned, and Briancourt was brought before the judges.

His evidence was damning, for he told his story in a straightforward and convincing manner. He explained how, after Sainte-Croix had hidden in the fireplace with the intention of stealing out when he was asleep and killing him, he had gone to the Lawyer Bocager, who had obtained for him his post with the Brinvilliers family. He had told this man what was happening in the household of his mistress, and asked Bocager to pass on this information to the President of the Courts, so that action might be taken and the deaths of two innocent women be averted.

Bocager had answered that he did not wish to hear such secrets, and advised the tutor to keep what he knew to himself. He promised that, if Briancourt returned quietly to the Hôtel d'Aubray and stayed there until a new situation could be found for him, that would be his wisest course.

He had done this, but later something Marie had said to him made him realize that Bocager had told her of the tutor's disclosures.

Briancourt's evidence went on: there was an attempt to assassinate him when pistols were fired at him in the street. He had returned to Bocager who had told him that there were too many people of importance involved in this affair for a simple tutor to think he could go against them.

Briancourt had been perplexed and had still been considering what he ought to do when he heard of Sainte-Croix's death and the flight of the Marquise de Brinvilliers.

When Marie was brought face to face with the tutor in the court she abused him as a liar and a drunkard; and boldly she faced her judges. But all her brave defiance could not save her. She was clearly guilty and was condemned to die.

*   *   *

The Abbé Edmé Pirot, a man of deep compassion, was assigned to help her through the difficult days to come. As a pious man, he deplored the terrible crimes she had committed and determined to bring her to a mood of repentance before she died.

Marie listened calmly to what he had to say, and, as calmly to him, eventually she made her confession.

Her confession seems to have been made not in fear. Marie was not afraid, although it is true that at this time she did not know that she was to be tortured before death. Marie was completely arrogant to the end; she repudiated the confession she had written in Liège to the last because she continued to believe that she could outwit her judges; when she was condemned, and not until then, did she confess the truth to Pirot.

Her pride is clearly shown when, having been taken to the torture chamber, the sentence of the court was read to her. Found guilty of the murder of her father and brothers she was condemned to make the 'amende honorable' before the door of Notre Dame; she was to be taken to the Cathedral in a tumbril, her feet naked and a rope about her neck, and there she would declare her sins. From thence she would be conducted to the Place de Grève to be beheaded when her body would be burnt and her ashes scattered. But, before she was executed, she was to suffer the terrible torture of the Questions Ordinary and Extraordinary in the hope that she would reveal the names of her accomplices. Having heard this sentence she was not thrown into a panic by the thought of death and the hideous torture which was to precede it, but she was furious at the indignity of having to make the amende honorable which was a public penance. That one of her rank should be forced to ride barefoot in a tumbril seemed to her such degradation that she temporarily disregarded the rest of the sentence, while she announced her anger that she should be so treated, and deplored the disgrace to her family.

At least if Marie was indifferent to the deaths of others, she was not as concerned, as most people would have been, at the prospect of her own.

* * *

The Marquis de Brinvilliers seemed to show little concern during his wife's trial. Not once did he visit her. Indeed he did not come to Paris.

When the Abbé commented on this, Marie defended her husband, declaring that he would have been there had he not been afraid of his creditors.

It seems strange that she who had always despised him should have defended him at this time. It may have been that she was loath to admit his indifference. She had suffered great humiliation over the affair of Desgrez, for she had believed him to be infatuated with her, and it must have been a great shock to her vanity to learn that he was merely feigning his infatuation in order to get her arrested and deported. As such women do, who are inordinately proud of their physical attractions and see themselves as femmes fatales, she felt the need to impress even the Abbé Pirot with her powers of attraction, and she could not bear that he should think for a moment that even a husband, who had been notoriously unfaithful, was at heart indifferent to her.

Marie's character did not change during the ordeal through which she now passed, nor did it when she came face to face with an even more terrible one.

I believe that her vanity, which had been her undoing, was to sustain her in the dark torture chambers of the Conciergerie and later on the Place de Grève.

*   *   *

Although she had confessed, it was decided to put her to the torture, for her trial had aroused great interest throughout France, and there was now a strong determination to discover the names of all those who had been concerned in the mysterious poison drama.

She was conducted to the chamber of pain, and the order was read to her. In spite of all the suffering she had caused to others, surely those men must have felt sorry for her. She was such a little woman, so dainty and feminine; and although she must have been very frightened, even in that dreary place she is said to have given no sign.

What were her thoughts when she saw the executioner and his assistant who were there to inflict the torture? Did she consider the violent agonies she had inflicted on others? I do not think this would occur to her. The poisoner never puts himself into the place of his victim, for how could he proceed if he did so? He never connects himself with the sufferings of others. She would look at the instruments of torture and think of nothing but the harm they were going to bring to her. But cowardice was not one of her characteristics any more than it was of Cesare's. Cesare died fighting bravely; she would die as bravely.

The two forms of torture mainly used in France during the seventeenth century were those of the Boot and the Water. In the first the legs were fitted into cases which were so tightly bound that they would not give. Wedges were then driven in to these 'Boots', the bones being crushed to make room for them. Four wedges were used in the *Question Ordinaire*; eight in the *Question Extraordinaire*. Those who underwent the torture of the Boot were rarely able to walk again.

The Water Torture was applied to Marie. She was stripped and her feet tied to rings in the floor. She was then forced backwards while her wrists were tied to rings in the wall. Her body was then bound to a bench two feet high. A horn was placed in her mouth and she was forced to drink the contents

of four jars of water, about twelve pints in all. Owing to
the acutely painful position of the body and the distension
of the stomach by the water, one of the most agonizing pains
conceivable was produced, and few could endure it without
being ready to do anything to have the torture stopped. That
was the *Question Ordinaire*. But Marie had been sentenced to
receive the *Question Extraordinaire*, so the bench to which she
was tied was removed and replaced by one more than a foot
higher. This position was even more painful, and her hands and
feet bled where the ropes cut into them. She was made to drink
the contents of four more jars while her tormentors urged her to
disclose the names of her accomplices.

Her courage was amazing. She had merely looked at the
jars and asked how such a little person as herself could swallow
so much water; and when the torture began she merely
murmured that they were killing her.

And when at length they released her she had told them
nothing more than she had told them before.

She was left lying, half dead, on a mattress in front of a fire.

*   *   *

Many of the ladies and gentlemen of the Court witnessed the
amende honorable and the execution of the Marquise de Brinvilliers. Madame de Sévigné was present, and mentions the
incident in her letters to her daughter. There is a report from
another source that English ladies of the best quality drove out
to see her end. These English ladies were no doubt Lady
Castlemaine and her friends, for she was in Paris at the time and
it is certain that a woman of her type would have found the
spectacle irresistible.

Most of those who were directly concerned had slipped
quietly away from Paris when Sainte-Croix had died. Christopher Glaser had disappeared at that time, giving up the
brilliant career which he was carving for himself in Paris. He
was not heard of again, which is very strange, since he was one
of the cleverest chemists of his day.

But there must have been many in the crowd, who had done
business with Sainte-Croix, to wonder whether their names
had been betrayed by Madame de Brinvilliers.

She was deprived of her shoes and stockings and made to
wear a white chemise; a white cap was put on her head and,
when she was led out to a roughly constructed cart, her pride
revolted that she—the Marquise de Brinvilliers—should be
driven to Notre Dame, barefoot and naked but for a chemise, in
this common cart. But she must submit. Exhausted by her

ordeal in the torture chamber, she yet retained her dignity
as she knelt on the steps leading to the porch; and there was a
silence among the noisy spectators as she repeated the words:

"I admit that wickedly and for vengeance I poisoned my
father and my brothers. I attempted to poison my sister-in-
law. I did this in order to possess myself of their property,
and for it I ask pardon of God, of the King, and of Justice."

The *amende honorable* over, the time had come to proceed to
the Place de Grève.

*   *   *

All the streets in the neighbourhood of the Place de Grève
were crowded with sightseers; the bell of the Tour d'Horloge
tolled dismally at intervals; and the tumbril in which Marie
sat, Pirot beside her, made its slow way from Notre Dame to the
Place de Grève.

Marie was going to her death, and the people shouted their
pleasure to see her brought low; they reminded her of her
crimes as she took her last ride; yet what distressed her even
more than riding thus in her humiliation was the fact that,
behind her cart to guard her, was a man whom she hated with
all the fierceness of her nature, so that, even with death so close,
she could be aware of him. She begged the priest who was in
the cart with her to move to one side so as to blot out the sight
of the police agent, Desgrez.

Her hatred of the man seems out of all proportion to the part
he played in her story. It was true that he had been the one to
bring her back to Paris, but I do not believe that her intense
dislike of him was due to that fact. She displayed no anger
against her judges or those who had borne witness against her;
nor did she show resentment towards the men who had tortured her. I think that her overwhelming vanity—which was
the key to her character—is displayed once more in her attitude
towards Desgrez.

She hated him, not so much because he had brought her back
to justice, but because she had tried to fascinate him and he had
refused to be fascinated.

And as she came to the place of execution, Desgrez was
close by to witness the completion of his work.

The crowd roared its approval, seeing her on the scaffold,
beside which were the faggots waiting for her headless body.
The faggots were being sprinkled with tar to make them burn
more fiercely, but Marie did not seem to notice this.

Her hair was loosened and the executioner cut it, slowly and laboriously as though he were pandering to the delight of the crowd which was longing for the supreme moment, yet loth to see the end of the spectacle. In her letters to her daughter, Madame de Sévigné comments on this and declares it to be an additional torture.

Marie stood up and for the last time felt the faint breeze which blew off the Seine, for the last time saw the majestic, blackened towers of Notre Dame.

Then a bandage was put over her eyes; her head was cut off and her tiny body cast into the tar and faggots.

*   *   *

A few days later Pennautier was released. He was so rich and powerful that he was able to save himself, and was exonerated completely. He lived thirty years longer than Marie and during that lifetime attained many honours.

The case of the Marquise de Brinvilliers was not forgotten; and it was soon after her death and the trial of the infamous La Voisin—that poisoner as notorious as Marie herself—in which members of the Court were involved, that it became a law in France that a poison-book should be kept by all apothecaries, so that there should be a record of those who had bought poisons. It is interesting to note that it was almost two hundred years later before this rule became law in England; but then, there were never great poison scandals in England as there had been in France and Italy, and one wonders whether this is due to the national temperament.

*   *   *

It is reported that a few minutes before she died, Marie said to her executioner: "Why is it that, when so many are guilty, I am the only one to die?"

This is a question which was no doubt asked by the spectators. So urgently was it asked that, immediately after her body had been thrown to the flames, the fickle crowd, which had so recently reviled her, spoke of her as though she were a saint taking the punishment of others who had sinned as deeply as she had.

There is no doubt that Sainte-Croix had helped others to remove the unwanted from their paths; it was for this reason that he had taken the room in the Place Maubert; and I wonder whether, if it were possible to know as much of the lives of those poisoners as it is about that of Madame de Brinvilliers, we should find those traits which are apparent in Marie and

Cesare: The arrogance, the indifference to others, the magnified picture of self, the minimized picture of the rest of the world, that peculiar blindness which cannot see the world as it is but only as a terrain for their own egoistic designs.

Marie and Cesare shared in common the fatal characteristics of the murderer.

DR. PRITCHARD

———————

My THIRD case brings me nearer to modern times, to the days when it was less easy to commit murder, when human life was considered of greater value than in the preceding centuries, and consequently when the murderer must employ greater cunning if he were to escape justice.

Dr. Edward William Pritchard seems as far removed from Cesare Borgia and Madame de Brinvilliers as does nineteenth-century Glasgow from fifteenth-century Rome and seventeenth-century Paris.

Edward Pritchard was born in Southsea on the 6th December of the year 1825; his father was a Captain in the Royal Navy. It was decided that he should enter the medical profession, and when he was fifteen years old he was sent to Portsmouth to study with two surgeons who were practising in that town.

As he came from a seafaring family it seemed natural that he should go into that service where his father, the Captain, could use his influence; he also had other relatives who held high positions in the Navy, including two who were said to be Admirals.

From the beginning of his career, Edward must have felt himself to be in a special position, and to have relished this; for he was by nature indolent, and it may have been that in these earlier days he began to feel that, since he was Edward Pritchard, he was born to be privileged and the fruits of success should fall naturally into his hands while others, lacking his advantages, must be expected to climb for them.

He was eventually gazetted as assistant-surgeon in Her Majesty's Navy, and in November 1846 was posted to H.M.S. *Victory*.

Edward was favoured in more ways than one, for in addition to his family connections he was exceptionally handsome. He had an air of distinction which came not only from his impressive height—he was six feet tall, and in those days, it is, I think, agreed, that the race was on average shorter than today—but from his handsome face. He had an aquiline nose, a large and beautifully shaped mouth, a luxuriant near-golden beard and a clean shaven upper lip, and his eyes were startling; they were penetrating, glittering, and they proclaimed not only his satisfaction with himself, but his determination to make everyone, with whom he came into contact, equally satisfied. His manner was even more attractive than his appearance. He flattered women not only with somewhat grandiloquent compliments, but with his admiring glances, in which he managed to convey that they aroused in him such desire that only his perfect manners prevented him from expressing it.

From H.M.S. *Victory* Edward passed to H.M.S. *Collingwood*, *Calypso*, and *Asia*. By 1850 he was serving in *Hecate*, and it was at this time that he made the acquaintance of Mary Jane Taylor.

Mary Jane was on a visit to Portsmouth from her home in Edinburgh, and she must have found the social round in Portsmouth very gay after the quiet life she had lived with her family. Her father, Mr. Michael Taylor, was a silk merchant of very comfortable means, but, living her sheltered life, Mary Jane had met few young men; there had never been any offer of marriage, one presumes—or at least none which was acceptable to the Taylors—and it may have been that they felt that in Portsmouth where Mary Jane's uncle, Dr. David Cowan, was well known in Navy circles, there might be a chance of the girl's meeting more eligible men than in her native city. Moreover her Uncle David could be trusted to introduce her to the right people.

Dr. David Cowan was an ex-surgeon of the Royal Navy who had become Superintendent Surgeon of Portsmouth Dockyard. He was a widower and apparently a jovial man who liked plenty of society, and when he retired he had remained in Portsmouth, a town in which he could keep in touch with many of his friends and lead a life not so very different from that which he had enjoyed in the past.

He must have been delighted to have Mary Jane with him and, being a kindly man, as well as a gay one, and understanding Mary Jane's shyness and that acute fear of the unmarried girl of that era that she might fail to find a husband, determined to bring her out and get her married.

Hecate was in port and there was to be a ball in one of the assembly halls; to this, Dr. David Cowan decided to take his niece.

This ball proved to be a fatal occasion in the life of Mary Jane Taylor, for it was here that she met Edward Pritchard. They danced together and presumably indulged in an interesting conversation, for the next day Edward called at the house of Dr. Cowan; so already plans must have been forming in Edward's head, for in those days young men did not make ceremonial calls unless they had intentions of some sort; and in a town like Portsmouth, if Edward had had intentions other than honourable, he would not have called on a young lady who was the niece of such a man as Dr. David Cowan.   •

The attraction Mary Jane felt for Edward is easy to understand; that of Edward for Mary Jane is more complicated.

There can be little doubt that Mary Jane must have begun to feel apprehensive that she would never find a husband; she must have visualized slipping into that state of which her world would feel overpoweringly contemptuous. In the middle of last century there were few people who were treated so slightingly as 'the old maid', as they labelled her; and it was possible, at that time, to qualify for that title in the middle twenties. It was a man's world; and it was generally accepted that if a woman had no husband there could be only one reason for it: no man had asked her to marry him! It was inconceivable to the masculine mind, and to many feminine ones, that any woman—unless she were very eccentric indeed—could fail to hope for a husband. Women in those days were so shackled by man-made conventions, that they found it difficult, and almost impossible, to stand out against them. Few ever thought of doing so, and it never entered their heads to question why a woman's fortune should become her husband's on marriage. The clever women were those who worked secretly and subtly to control their men. Many succeeded in doing this, but although it provided them with personal triumphs, it did nothing to alleviate the state of servitude to the male in which the rest of the female world was immersed. In this hypocritical age men went on their knees to propose, but women were on theirs very soon afterwards. It is this hypocrisy—largely imported to England by the Prince Consort—which makes me feel that the nineteenth century was one of the most sinister of all times, an age in which much secret cruelty was practised behind a façade of piety and respectability.

It is interesting to speculate on how many women, but for this ridiculous convention, would have remained unmarried because they preferred that state, and whether Mary Jane Taylor would have been one of them.

In view of this prevalent opinion it is to be presumed that Mary Jane Taylor, while she may have felt very apprehensive, was at the same time relieved that at last there was a chance of avoiding that despised condition and attaining the honour of being chosen to share bed and board with, and give up her fortune to, one of the master sex.

As for Edward, why did he, who must have had his successes with women, decide to make that call on somewhat insignificant Mary Jane Taylor?

In view of his future adventures, it is hardly likely that he would be attracted by a girl like Mary Jane—except for one thing. That which was flamboyant in Edward would surely have looked for some equally flamboyant quality in women; he must have been more interested in the obviously attractive women from whom he could expect a sexual response. Mary Jane's picture shows a modest woman, completely innocent, a woman of gentle character and upbringing; and as no doubt she would have been aware of the disgrace of remaining unmarried, she would also have been brought up either in complete ignorance of what would be expected of her in the marriage bed, or to regard this as something to which she must dutifully submit. It would be quite unpleasant, not to be thought of during the day time and only indulged in under cover of darkness, but to be met with in that quiet and unquestioning wifely submission, because the ways of God and the superior sex were not understood by a mere woman. Edward would have sensed this in Mary Jane. He was a man of strong sensual needs; he required companions in amorous adventures who would be prepared to offer him a passion equal to his own.

Why then was he attracted by Mary Jane?

Because Mary Jane possessed characteristics which were necessary in the woman he would make his wife. She quite clearly believed all that he told her of himself, and was ready to regard him as he wished to be seen. To Mary Jane the tall, handsome and charming Edward Pritchard was the Edward Pritchard the young doctor showed the world, and he could look into Mary Jane's eyes and see himself mirrored there—the infinitely desirable husband. In Mary Jane he sensed awe and respect, and he knew that she would be easy to dominate; she was soft and gentle, and during their married life she would be his to command. She would accept all that he wished her to accept—and without question; and as it was impossible for a man of his tastes to give up habits which had become normal with him, he must have a wife who could be easily duped into believing the stories he told her.

There was another reason. Dr. Cowan was a man of influence, and men of Edward's type have a deep reverence for influence. Some instinct tells them that they can never attain their ambitions by their own efforts, and they dupe themselves into believing that the way to success is through kind friends and relations—those men and women of influence.

So, in the year 1850, Dr. Edward Pritchard called at the house of Dr. David Cowan and—because it *was* the year 1850—from that moment his intentions were obvious.

Later that year the wedding took place, and after the honeymoon Edward returned to *Hecate*, and there was nothing for Mary Jane to do but go back to her parents in Edinburgh.

Mary Jane must have been very contented at that time, for the Taylor home was a very happy one, and she could live in it as she had as a young girl, but with the additional comfort which the ability to dispense with that fear of being an 'old maid' brought her.

Mrs. Taylor and her husband were anxious for their daughter's welfare and they thought it most unwise for husband and wife to live long apart. It would be much more satisfactory if Edward had a practice in some town not too far from Edinburgh; so they began to look about for one that they might secure for their son-in-law.

*   *   *

Eventually a practice was found in the Yorkshire town of Hunmanby, so Edward left the Navy and set up house there.

Edward found the life of general practitioner less suited to his character than that of ship's doctor; and it could not have been long before he began to hanker for the old life. But Edward was a man determined to enjoy what he had. This was because he lived largely in a world of the imagination where he was a superman, many times the size of his fellow human beings who seemed poor creatures in comparison with himself; and it was not long before the inhabitants of Hunmanby began to be not only insignificant but unpleasant.

To meet a charming woman in some port of call, to enjoy a brief love affair, to tell her of his great achievements in his native country—that was delightful; and the lady accepted his story. Why should she not? Edward told his stories with such plausibility, because while he told them he believed them himself.

It was different in Hunmanby, for that town, situated between Scarborough and Bridlington, is in Yorkshire, and the people of Yorkshire pride themselves on their honest outlook, their bluntness and their sharp rejection of humbug.

The doctor, because of his charm, soon secured a large practice; but the people of Hunmanby were not gullible. They

had soon caught him telling lies about himself and his travels;
they had branded him as unreliable.

But at first Edward prospered and was able to acquire an
additional practice in Filey; he was appointed Medical
Officer for the district of Bridlington; he produced a guide-
book on the beauties of the neighbourhood and wrote articles
which were published in local journals; he gave lectures on the
strange places he had visited, and if he had never visited some
of these places, except in his imagination—well, his imagination was a lively one. He felt really angry when his veracity
was questioned. He *believed* the stories he told, and it seemed to
him insulting that others should doubt his word.

In the local club he liked to discourse on politics, and the
Crimean War gave him opportunities of exploiting his eloquence. It also brought his arrogance into the limelight, for
there must have been many divided opinions on Palmerston's
actions.

During the six years he and Mary Jane were at Hunmanby
four children were born to them: Jane Frances, who was called
Fanny, Charles, Horace and Kenneth. These children adored
their father. Edward could never resist admiration and he was
by nature fond of children. They doted on him; he doted on
them; and this was a source of great pleasure to Mary Jane.

She herself had not been well since the coming of little
Fanny, the eldest; and the births of the others, following in
quick succession, had not improved her health. She suffered
acutely from headaches and some affliction of the eyes. Her
mother, delighted with her grandchildren, and anxious about
her daughter's health, kept a sharp watch on the family,
visiting Hunmanby often and insisting on Mary Jane's returning to Edinburgh at frequent intervals to enjoy her native air.

Mrs. Taylor thought Edward charming. He was always
tender to Mary Jane and solicitous concerning her health. It
was such a comfort to have a doctor in the family; she would
understand and appreciate this now that her own son Michael
was also in the medical profession.

Edward must have been delighted that Mary Jane should
visit her family so often, because it would have given him scope
to continue his amorous adventures; but so certain did he
become that he could conduct these with his own brilliant
cleverness, that he grew a little careless.

One day a very charming young woman came to the surgery,
and Edward was immediately excited by her. He enjoyed
examining attractive young women and he found it stimulating
to discover how far he could go in these little surgery flirtations.

They seemed doubly enthralling because this was the sort of conduct which was frowned on by the profession and which, if it came to the ears of some, could put an end to his career.

But Edward was so sure of himself; he would have been confident that he could tell at a glance which women were to be trusted to play his game; and if he made a mistake—well he could always rely on his charm to extricate him. He was completely assured of his ability in that direction.

He clearly misjudged this particular woman, for when she understood his intentions she protested vigorously. Edward would have been furious, for he always saw everything from his own point of view. His pride would have been deeply hurt and he would immediately think of the woman as a prudish idiot and a stupid creature. But he must have experienced some alarm, for the woman told him that she would go straight home and inform her husband of his unprofessional conduct.

It had happened at last. He had run into danger and was caught. He had been a little too sure of himself; he must have felt extremely apprehensive.

During the rest of the day when he was with his family, surely he wondered what would happen to them all if this woman kept her promise and with her husband made a scandal. They could so easily do this, and he must have thought that there would be many people in the town only too ready to believe any such charge brought against him. He would think of his enemies as jealous people, mostly men who envied him his adventures, his ability to hold an audience with stories of them, and, of course, his success with women.

He would have been jerked out of his dreams and forced to see the Edward Pritchard whom some others saw, and who was quite different from that man with whom his family were so familiar; and the fact that the Taylors were so devoted to their daughter—and so interested in everything that concerned her— would have increased his alarm. These Taylors would not let Mary Jane alone; they clucked over her as though she were still their chick. It would have been typical of Edward that, although in the past he had been glad of the Taylors' devotion to their daughter, now that he saw a possible inconvenience in this, he would deplore it.

As far as Mrs. Taylor was concerned, he could manage *her*. She was only a woman and he despised her; he could charm her, not by telling her how attractive she was, but by discussing her ailments, and telling her that there was no harm in her taking her doses of Battley's Sedative Solution for her headaches, although of course her son Michael—that prim young doctor who liked to talk shop with Edward, sometimes to Edward's discomfiture—would have told her not to use the stuff, which contained laudanum or opium. He was not afraid of Mrs. Taylor; it was the men of the family whom he suspected of not being quite so fond of him as the ladies were. Old Mr. Taylor, the silk merchant, was shrewd; so was Michael, the doctor.

And what would happen if there was a scandal, he must have tried to imagine; and such thoughts would certainly have kept him awake at nights.

His fears proved too well founded, for the day after the incident had occurred, the woman's husband appeared at the surgery and demanded to see Edward. He was a man many years older than his wife, of choleric temper and clearly determined to have his revenge. He told Edward he was a scoundrel, and assured him that he would be hearing more of this disgraceful affair.

Exposure seemed imminent, and Edward must have been frantic with anxiety; but he would have remained outwardly calm, outwardly assured that God, Providence, Fate or his Guardian Angel would never allow a man of his ability and usefulness to the world, to be ruined for such a small matter as this.

With great presence of mind he despatched Mary Jane to Edinburgh, suggesting that she take the children with her for a change of air; but even a man who believed that special privileges were due to him to the extent that Edward must have done, would have been unnerved during the days which followed.

Edward's truly astonishing luck on this occasion must have made him feel that he really did enjoy the divine protection which he was accustomed to call upon when he was in any difficulty.

He learned suddenly, when it appeared that there was certain to be a prosecution, that the husband of the woman whom he had insulted, had died suddenly.

In view of this the case was dropped.

*   *   *

To some it might have sounded too good to be true; not so to Edward. But he had to face the fact that it was going to be unpleasant staying in Yorkshire where too many people knew of the affair.

The strain of the incident had affected his health, and the Taylors, whom he managed to keep in ignorance of what had really happened, must have thought that he had been working too hard with one practice in Hunmanby and another in Filey in addition to his writing and lecturing. They were only too glad to have Mary Jane and the children to stay with them in Edinburgh while Edward took a post as medical attendant to a very rich man who was travelling for his health. So, having bought the diploma of Doctor of Medicine *in absentia* from Erlangen University, and becoming a Licentiate of the Society of Apothecaries in London, he left England and spent some months in Egypt and the Holy Land.

By the time he returned, a new practice had been found for him. This was in Glasgow—within easy reach of the Taylors in Edinburgh.

*   *   *

His recent experiences had not made him more modest. He was eager to talk of his adventures and sought every opportunity to lecture. His imagination was given full flight and, seeing all those about him as pigmies, he often exaggerated to such an extent that he soon earned the general reputation of being a liar; and when he tried to gain admittance to the Faculty of Physicians and Surgeons he could find no one ready to propose him. He tried for the vacant Chair of Surgery at the Andersonian University, declaring that he had had many opportunities in almost every part of the world of gaining experience. He failed to impress, and assuring himself that a man of his calibre must inspire envy in the less gifted, contented himself with becoming a member of the Glasgow Athenaeum and lecturing whenever he could.

He was often snubbed by the members of the Athenaeum who soon began to wish that he had not been elected. He was openly told that many of his stories of the adventures which had befallen him could not be true; he did not care. He would not see himself as these people saw him. He was blatantly in love with himself and may have believed, at least while he told them, that all the exciting and heroic escapades which he declared had befallen him were true.

In the year 1860, when Edward had been travelling abroad, Giuseppe Garibaldi had joined the Piedmontese against the Austrians and helped in the overthrow of the Kingdom of Naples in the hope of uniting the whole of Italy under Victor Emmanuel.

Garibaldi was popular in Britain, and Edward seemed to have become fascinated by the adventures of the Italian patriot; he began to boast that during his travels he had met the great Italian and that they had become friends. He even went so far as to have an inscription engraved on a walking stick, which ran: "Presented by General Garibaldi to Edward William Pritchard." But the cane was known to have been in Edward's possession long before the inscription had been put on it, and at the Club that scorn for his mendacious arrogance increased.

Edward Pritchard wished to be recognized as a great man; he saw himself as a great man; and he was prepared to go to all sorts of stupid subterfuge to make people accept him on his own valuation. I think it is very probable that there was an abnormality in his character which made him believe that his dreams were realities. In Edward's world there was only Edward, looming above all others; the insignificant creatures who made up the rest of the world were of no importance whatsoever; they had been given their existence merely to minister to Edward's comfort and pleasure.

It seems incredible, too, that he should have taken photographs of himself to a local shop and asked that they should be displayed, for sale, in the window. But this is what he did. He made a habit, also, of carrying them about with him and giving them to casual acquaintances such as fellow-travellers on trains.

*   *   *

On the night of the 5th May in the year 1863 there occurred the first of the suspicious happenings in the life of this man.

We have no proof of what is supposed to have happened on that occasion, as here again Edward enjoyed that phenomenal luck which saved him from justice and thereby cost the lives of two people. It was only later when his conduct became a matter of great public concern that the mysterious happenings of this night were recalled.

On this 5th of May there was a fire at Edward's house. He was then living at No. 11 Berkeley Terrace. In the fire a young servant girl named Elizabeth M'Girn lost her life. She was found in her bed, and the extraordinary fact was discovered that she had made no attempt to escape but had lain there as though sleeping, while she was burned to death.

The newspapers of the times reported the incident in detail, describing the house at Berkeley Terrace in Berkeley Street as one consisting of two stories and attics, the attics being the sleeping quarters of the servants. A constable noticed the fire through the window of the attic and at once rang the doorbell.

Dr. Pritchard appeared and said that he had been awakened by his two sons, who slept in the room next to his on the second floor; the two boys had been disturbed by the smell of smoke

and the sound of crackling flames. It was immediately apparent
to the doctor that the house was on fire so he took the boys down
to the hall and then ran up to the attic calling the servant by
her name. There was no answer and the top floor was so full
of smoke that it was impossible for the doctor to go further.
As he ran downstairs in order to raise the alarm, the constable
rang the doorbell.

Dr. Pritchard then explained to the constable what was
happening and together they returned to the top floor, and as
they were unable to enter the girl's bedroom, they hurried
down to give the alarm. The central engine station received
this by telegraph from the Anderson Police Office and when
the brigade eventually arrived and made their way to the attic,
after extinguishing the flames, they found the servant dead in
the bed, her body severely charred.

She was lying on her back, her left arm by her side, her right
arm in a bent position. The arm, from elbow to hand, was
completely consumed; the head was also charred, but the
girl's limbs, on account of their being covered by blankets, were
almost untouched.

When he returned from his rounds on Monday night, Dr.
Pritchard saw the light in the servant's room but he did not
call her to enquire if anyone had come to the house to ask for
him. He went to the boys' room to make sure that they were
safely in bed; then he himself retired. The time was twelve
o'clock.

It was pointed out that Elizabeth M'Girn often read in bed;
and the theory was put forward that the bedclothes had caught
alight, and as the fire had started at the head of the bed, the
bed-hangings may have come into contact with the gas jet.
The explanation of the fire seemed simple enough; what was
not so easy to understand was why the girl had made no
attempt to escape. It seemed certain that she must have been
suffocated while asleep, for the position in which her body had
been found clearly showed that she had made no effort to
move.

Her fellow-servant had not been at home on the fatal night,
having accompanied the mistress of the house on a visit. The
house was badly damaged but this was covered by insurance.

Thus the newspaper accounts.

It was true that the house was insured but, when Edward
claimed insurance for valuable articles of jewellery, the
insurance company, since there was no trace of such jewellery
in the debris, showed signs of becoming inquisitive. Edward
quickly revised his claim, and accepted a very small portion of

what he had first demanded, and seemed eager to let the matter drop. It was dropped and forgotten until some years later when, in view of what was known of Edward's character, a more sinister theory of what had happened at the time of the fire in Berkeley Terrace was put forth.

The theory is that the fire was arranged to remove Elizabeth M'Girn from his path, because Elizabeth was becoming a nuisance. It is not unreasonable to assume a set of circumstances which would give rise to this situation.

Edward was living in a small house with Mary Jane, the four children and two servants. One of these servants was a young girl: Elizabeth M'Girn.

There can be no doubt that Mary Jane had ceased to attract him physically—even if she ever had. Mary Jane's health had been poor since the birth of the first child; we discover that she suffered constantly from her eye affliction and bad headaches. It is almost certain that Edward was constantly looking about him for new mistresses, and there in his own house was a lusty young girl—at least one may presume that she was lusty and willing, for one cannot imagine Edward's stooping to pay prolonged court to a servant girl. It seems certain that Elizabeth M'Girn became his mistress.

Some complications had arisen. We do not hear that Elizabeth was pregnant, so it may have been that she had become insolent to the doctor. I think this is the more likely. If she were pregnant, as a doctor he would have been able to deal with that, and it would not have presented a motive for murder. Perhaps Elizabeth was attempting to blackmail him in her clumsy way, threatening to tell Mary Jane of the relationship between them unless she was treated with more consideration; she may even have asked for money.

Although Mary Jane was completely under Edward's domination, I feel sure that he would have been determined to keep from her the knowledge of his philanderings with the servant. He was always eager to preserve his dignity.

He may have pictured Mary Jane, confiding in her family regarding his infidelity. He might have imagined the anger of Mr. Taylor, the scorn of Michael and the grief of Mrs. Taylor.

It was unthinkable that he should be exposed.

Edward had come up against a situation which involved either discomfort to himself or the need for the elimination of the cause of the discomfort; and, true to his type, Edward saw only one way out.

He would say to himself: "But who is this woman? A servant girl? Quite unimportant in the world! *She* to try to ruin *my* life!"

There was only one solution for a man of Edward's kind: her removal.

There are three facts which must be remembered. The first: On that May night, Mary Jane was not at home. She may have gone to Edinburgh to see her family, and she had taken two of the children and the other servant with her. The two boys remained with their father. Edward no doubt felt he would be capable of looking after them. They occupied an apartment next to his own, so he could make sure they were safe. The most important people to get out of the house would be Mary Jane and the other servant. Why should he not suggest a visit to Edinburgh?

"You are looking tired, my love." One imagines his saying this with that solicitous charm for which Mary Jane was so grateful. "A little of your native air would do you good. You know it always does. For your health's sake, Mary Jane, I shall *insist* on your going."

Mary Jane would be eager to go. She was always eager to go to Edinburgh. The children would be pleased to see their grandparents; and the servant would surely be glad of the trip in the happy company of Mary Jane and the children.

Thus Edward would have the house clear of all those who might make difficulties.

The second: When he came in that night, as he had admitted to the Glasgow reporter, he had not summoned the servant to discover if there were any calls for him. Why not? The first thing a doctor would ask on coming in would normally be: "Has anyone called?" Yet why did he not do so on this night?

He probably did ask, and if there had been any calls decided to ignore them, having a more important task to perform.

The third: Why was it that the girl was found in her bed lying naturally as though she were sleeping? Why had she lain still while the fire scorched and burned her body? There is only one reason why a girl should do this. It was because she was unable to do anything else. She would have been suffocated by smoke, but surely before she became unconscious through it, she would have awakened, realized what was happening and made some movement?

I suggest she was drugged.

I imagine Edward's coming home that day. Mary Jane was away and the only people in the house were Edward, Elizabeth and the two boys—who would already have been in bed as it was eleven o'clock when Edward said he had come home; as this could be verified, it is hardly likely that he would lie on this point.

I imagine Elizabeth M'Girn, meeting him in the hall—in the drawing-room perhaps. I imagine her veiled insolence, the implicit refusal to be treated as a servant now that she was his mistress.

He would have his plan ready, for he must have prepared it. Otherwise why were Mary Jane and the others away on this night? One can imagine the suave charm with which he would lightly cover that acquiescence which he wanted to show her, to lull her fears. What more likely than that he should unlock the cabinet and offer her a glass of wine? He would choose the moment to slip a strong dose of some sedative into the drink. Perhaps he had already prepared this in readiness. He would know exactly how much was needed to put her into a drugged sleep; he would know exactly what to use without arousing suspicion, and what effect it would have.

I picture their lifting the glasses and drinking—Edward smiling resignedly, letting her believe that he considered the physical satisfaction she was capable of giving him was worth the surrender of his dignity. I picture Elizabeth, emptying her glass in defiant triumph, telling herself that by her cleverness she would make a comfortable little place for herself, for she had the master exactly where she wanted him.

There would follow an amorous scene, during which he would tell her that he would visit her in her room, for it would be safer there. They must not run the risk of waking the boys who were sleeping in the room next to his. It was probably because it was necessary to get Elizabeth into her own bed that he had kept the two boys from going with their mother. The affair would have been very difficult to stage if Elizabeth had insisted on sharing his bed, which she might well have done had the two little boys not been sleeping in the next room.

He would have suggested that Elizabeth should go to her room while he locked up and made sure that the boys were safely asleep.

This would seem very natural to Elizabeth and she would obey. In her bed she would have waited a little while perhaps, but only a little while before the drug began to take effect.

I picture the scene: Edward coming stealthily up to the attic and looking at the sleeping girl lying there in her drugged sleep, the girl who had thought to dictate to *him*, the foolish little servant girl who had tried to undermine the prestige and dignity of Edward Pritchard.

It would be about midnight, and he would have to wait awhile, for the fire would be seen through the attic window and he did not want it to be discovered too soon.

The house was quiet; the boys were peacefully sleeping. He would certainly have been a little anxious about the boys, for he dearly loved his children who repaid him by adoring him. He was always dear, kind Papa to them. No harm must come to the boys.

He would have started the fire between two and three o'clock. It must appear a natural accident, so it would begin near the gas jet. Elizabeth would be lying there, deep in her drugged sleep, unaware of the ominous crackle of flames, the acrid smell of the smoke. He would watch until the bed was well alight, and only a man with the vision of a murderer, with the mind of a murderer, seeing himself all-important and other human beings of no account at all, *could* have stood there and looked down on that drugged girl, knowing what would shortly happen to her.

Then down to the next floor to wait. There must be no alarm until the top floor was completely destroyed and Elizabeth M'Girn's body so charred as to be unrecognizable among the burning remains of the room.

He would stand alert, listening, acutely aware of the two precious lives in the adjoining apartment.

According to himself it was from the two little boys that he first learned of the fire. They had heard the crackling flames and smelt the smoke, and ran into his room to tell him so.

It must have been an earlier discovery than he had wished for, but he acted promptly. He took the boys by the hand and hurried them downstairs. Perhaps they reminded him of Elizabeth up there. However, he ordered them to stay where they were while he went up to call Elizabeth. He called her; he says in his account that he could not go up beyond the door because there was a barrier of flames and the smoke blinded him.

At that moment the policeman knocked at the door. Edward then explained how his sons had warned him, and that there was a girl asleep in the attic, and that he had already tried to reach her; he and the policeman then went upstairs, and by this time it really was impossible to reach Elizabeth. Even so the firemen must have arrived too soon for Edward's peace of mind, and the fire was extinguished too quickly to eliminate that evidence which afterwards seemed so damning: the fact that Elizabeth had made no attempt to escape from the burning room.

There is no proof that this happened in the way I have described it; but the incident was recalled later and the facts disclosed appeared then to have a very sinister significance; and as Dr. Pritchard, after having made claims on the insurance company which were questioned, suddenly decided to withdraw them and accept far less than he had originally asked, in his desire to stop enquiries, added to other extra-ordinary details, suggests that the above version is by no means implausible.

Edward showed later how ruthlessly he could act when he was in a difficult situation, how indifferent he was to the pain and suffering of those who had been dearer to him than a servant girl; and I think that, when Edward's story is con-sidered and Edward's character understood, it will be agreed that what happened on that early May morning at Berkeley Terrace must have been something on the lines I have suggested.

*   *   *

After the fire, No. 11 Berkeley Terrace was no longer habitable, and the family moved to No. 22 Royal Crescent.

Edward was no doubt very shaken over this affair, as he must have been over the lady patient of Hunmanby. Not that he would have given much thought to what he had done to Elizabeth M'Girn. That was a necessity and Elizabeth would be no more to him than a mouse invading the pantry. He had eliminated her, that was all. Like Cesare Borgia and Marie de Brinvilliers he was not in the least concerned with any stab of conscience.

But it must have been disconcerting to know that there had been dissatisfaction among the insurance people. He had been on his dignity with them, had made speeches to them, had written grandiloquent letters to them; but they must have shaken him badly. He had sensed danger close at hand; otherwise he would never have allowed people who had been— as he would put it—insolent to him over a petty matter of insurance, to have scored a victory.

He had seen the danger signals and naturally he had wanted no inquisitive people asking questions about Elizabeth M'Girn.

He must therefore have suffered some qualms; but it seems possible, in view of other risks which he took, that he had come to believe he was sacrosanct. He was godlike; he said: "You shall die!" and his victim died. The husband who had tried to ruin him had died. Elizabeth, who had tried to do likewise, had died, with a little help from him. Twice he had faced disaster and he had come triumphantly through. He was therefore convinced that, with him, all things were possible.

Installed in the new house it was necessary to acquire a new maid to fill the place of the unlucky Elizabeth M'Girn; and

there came to the house in Royal Crescent a fifteen-year-old
girl named Mary M'Leod.

Mary was a young girl from a poor home in Glasgow, very
delighted to get a job in a doctor's comfortable household.
Quiet, innocent, grateful, it was inevitable that she should
arouse Edward's interest from the moment she entered the
house, for she was so humble, so different from the girl who,
there was no doubt he would have persuaded himself by now,
had met a just fate. Such was Edward's nature that he would
have looked upon his horrible deed as an act of mercy; judging
from his letters one can quite believe that he would have convinced himself that by first drugging and then burning Elizabeth M'Girn to death, he had saved her from a life of sin. Well,
Mary resembled Elizabeth M'Girn in one thing only: there
was in Mary a sensuality as yet latent, which in the hands of
an expert could be gently aroused.

Little Mary M'Leod was doomed from the moment she
entered the Pritchard household.

Her photograph, taken with one of the children, shows her to
be a neat little girl, without beauty and without a great deal of
intelligence, but her attractiveness—and particularly to a man
like Edward—is immediately discerned. Mary M'Leod would
be easily subdued; she was clearly the sort of girl who should
have been married young, and she would have made a good
mother to a brood of children. She appears to be the sort of
girl who, once awakened to sexual passion, would be unable to
prevent herself indulging in it, no matter what the circumstances.

So from the moment of her entry into the household, poor
little Mary M'Leod began to attract the attentions of the
master of the house.

Mary arrived in Royal Crescent at Whitsuntide, and during
the summer, when Mary Jane took the children away for a
holiday, the fifteen-year-old girl became Edward's mistress.

*   *   *

The fire at Berkeley Terrace proved to be a great strain on
finances. Without doubt Edward prated about the dishonesties
of insurance companies, completely ignoring the fact that it
was himself who had brought the matter of insurance to a quick
conclusion.

The Taylors, no doubt realizing that their beloved Mary
Jane was not as comfortably off as they would have liked her to
be, were much concerned. Mrs. Taylor would naturally wish
her daughter to enjoy all the comforts to which she had been

accustomed. She had thought that marriage with a doctor would have brought these, but Edward had seemed to be unlucky so far. He was not like their son, Michael, who was going ahead in the medical profession. First the Hunmanby practice had not been a success, and Edward had left the place rather hurriedly, owing one or two debts. And no sooner had he appeared to be settled in Glasgow than there had been this disastrous fire, following which Edward had been so badly treated by the insurance people.'

I imagine Mrs. Taylor's having long talks with her husband and her son. The shrewd silk merchant was probably not so eager to help. Edward would seem to him somewhat unreliable and not very businesslike; and it is possible that Mr. Taylor would have had little patience with Edward.

But Mrs. Taylor was not thinking of Edward. Her thoughts would be all for Mary Jane. No doubt Mary Jane's father would point out that, if Mary Jane needed a rest, her home in Edinburgh was always waiting for her. Of course this was so, Mrs. Taylor would indignantly retort; but Mary Jane had her pride, and she did not believe that her daughter confided *all* her difficulties, even to her mother.

It was clear to Mrs. Taylor that the house in Royal Crescent was expensive. When she was in Glasgow she had seen a house for sale in Sauchiehall Street which would be ideal for Mary Jane's family.

And where, the shrewd Mr. Taylor would certainly have asked, could Edward find the money to put down for a house? From you! his wife would have told him.

A little persuasion, a few tears, a little anger about his indifference to their daughter's health, and Mr. Taylor did what Mrs. Taylor was determined he should do.

The cost of the house in Sauchiehall Street was £2,000. The Taylors arranged that £1,600 could be borrowed on the security of the house itself. They paid £400 down as purchase money, and Edward was handed £100 as a loan to help him over this difficult time. Then the family moved into the new home.

The house consisted of a basement, in which were two rooms, which served as servants' bedrooms, as well as a kitchen and a larder; on the ground floor were three rooms, two very large and one smaller which became the consulting room, the dining-room and the pantry. On the next floor were the drawing-room, two bedrooms and a small sitting-room; on the second floor two large bedrooms, a small one and the nursery.

There was plenty of room for the family, and to show his

parents-in-law that he was determined to get out of his financial difficulties, Edward decided to take two medical students to live in and study the profession. Shortly after a Mr. Connell and a Mr. King came to live with them.

The affair with Mary M'Leod was becoming more and more absorbing to Edward. He was finding the young servant girl delightful. It was difficult to conduct an affair of this nature in a household of so many people, but Edward was masterly at deceiving those about him. It would not have occurred to Mary Jane to suspect that the shy servant girl could be in the least attractive. The middle-aged servant, Catherine Lattimer, spent most of her time in the basement and, if Mary absented herself from the servants' quarters for long periods at a time, Catherine presumed she was on duty with the mistress.

However, Mary was ripe, and Edward found her so irresistible that he could not help taking risks; and one day Mary Jane opened one of the bedroom doors to find her husband there, and the servant with him. Mary was on the bed and the doctor was bending over her, kissing her.

Mary Jane, horrified, shut the door and hurried downstairs. Most men would have been somewhat nonplussed at being discovered in such an unmistakably compromising situation; but Edward, who had dealt with Elizabeth M'Girn and the insurance company in even more difficult circumstances, believed himself to be equal to dealing with poor Mary Jane. In the years of his marriage he had completely subdued her, and he would be certain that he could do so on this occasion.

Mary M'Leod continued to live in the house, which shows that Edward must have been able to offer some plausible explanation to Mary Jane for, submissive as she was, she would hardly have allowed the girl to remain if Edward had not convinced her of his innocence. It would have been so easy to have gone to the Taylors—to whom Edward owed money— and to have brought the wrath of the family on Edward's head. Moreover, it would have been the easiest thing possible for Mary Jane to take the children to Edinburgh. There would always be a warm welcome waiting for her there.

But she did not. And Mary M'Leod remained in the house, while Edward continued to be trusted.

Edward held great sway over Mary Jane. His gentle, rather silky manner—it exudes from his literary style in his letters and confessions—must have convinced her, and yet underlying it there is a touch of the sinister which must have frightened her. Mary Jane was a woman of weak character. She wanted to believe her husband faithful and that she had not made a mistake in marrying him; therefore she let herself believe in him. The house in Edinburgh must have seemed a haven of rest, but if she left Edward, she would go to it under a cloud of shame which, although less humiliating than remaining an 'old maid', would certainly bring reproach upon her. Moreover a wife of the 1860's was supposed to endure her husband's frailties in silence.

So Mary Jane would have trusted because she longed to.

Edward probably told her that she had been mistaken about the kisses. Mary was on the bed, yes; and they were in a bed-room. That could not be denied. But had his dear Mary Jane forgotten that he was a doctor, and that it was sometimes necessary for a doctor to examine a patient? The girl had asked for advice; was Mary Jane going to complain because he had given it? Was she going to get stupid ideas every time examina-tions took place? No! She was going to be his dear, sensible Mary Jane; and she was not going to make shameful sugges-tions which deeply shocked her husband and indeed made him wonder whether she was after all his pure sweet Mary Jane, since she could harbour such thoughts.

One imagines the scene: Mary Jane in tears, accusing her-self of folly—criminal folly—and begging Edward to forgive her. Edward would be magnanimous; I picture his lifting a cautionary finger to wag at her. It was a good thing, he would remind her, that she was possessed of a kindly husband, a husband who was ready to understand and explain.

Poor Mary Jane! When he had left her and the spell of his presence was no longer overpowering her, might she have said to herself: "But I did see them and they *were* kissing!"

*   *   *

Such unrestrained passion as that of Edward and Mary M'Leod gave rise to inevitable difficulties.

Mary became pregnant.

The young girl was probably terrified. She would imagine herself no longer a delight but a nuisance to the doctor; she would believe that she might be sent away, back in disgrace to the Glasgow tenement, to the poverty from which she had escaped. She believed that the doctor would deny that he had had anything to do with her condition, and of course everybody would believe a doctor's word against that of a poor servant girl.

In terror she would have gone to Edward; in trembling apprehension waited for his cold dismissal.

But this would be a situation such as Edward loved. This

little Mary, so enticing, so physically attractive, such a natural little animal—no foolish inhibitions, no holding back of real emotions—little Mary, ever ready, ever compliant, was on an occasion like this ready to accept her fate. She did not come to blackmail as Elizabeth M'Girn had done. Oh, how he must have thanked God that he had saved that girl—and her victims—from an evil life! No, Mary came humbly to tell him the truth, to wait, with frightened eyes, for the blows of misfortune.

I imagine this scene's taking place in the surgery where, owing to the counter-attractions of Mary, Edward was now behaving with decorum towards even the most beautiful of lady patients. Their beauty had little appeal. Most of them were cold and quite calculating when compared with Mary M'Leod; they would make conditions and they had nothing, with which to bargain, that he could not have from that soft little animal with the perfectly functioning body.

And now she was pregnant, and the poor child thought that was the end of all that was worth while in her life, because she believed it would mean the end of her relationship with Dr. Pritchard.

He would have drawn her to him and stroked back the rather coarse hair from the narrow brow. This had happened, he would murmur, and naturally it had frightened her. He understood her fear. He admitted that had this happened with some people there could be trouble . . . great trouble. And many a man would be eager to forget all the pleasure he had enjoyed because of this terrible catastrophe which had befallen her.

But he was not only her benevolent lover, employer, teacher in the arts of love. He was a doctor, and doctors were all-knowing, all-powerful. Matters such as this, when left in their capable hands, need cause no undue anxiety.

Edward was fond of her and she need have no fear. He would perform a little operation—nothing much—for she had been wise in telling him without delay; and in a little while he would work the miracle.

Mary would have looked at him, her childish eyes wide with wonder; she would have been unable to understand at once the meaning of her good fortune. She was not to be turned out; she was to stay here and the doctor would take care of everything. It seemed that instead of despising her, he was prepared to be kinder than ever before.

Those childish eyes would have been filled with adoration as she looked at him; and it may have been that adoration was the very thing which Edward sought from those about him.

From no one, apart from his young children, would he have received it in the same measure as he did from little Mary M'Leod. Mary Jane? He would have had it from her at first; but he was beginning to find Mary Jane tiresome. Submissive she might be, but now he had discovered Mary M'Leod who had all Mary Jane's submissiveness plus this desirable sexuality.

He may have thought at that time what a pleasant house this would be if there were no Mary Jane in it. If this girl could spend her nights with him in the big double bed in place of Mary Jane, how very satisfactory that would be. No need for stolen moments. No fear of scenes of discovery such as that in the bedroom when Mary Jane had come upon him kissing the girl! Such scenes were distressing to a man of his dignity.

The children were very fond of Mary M'Leod. Her sort had a way with children. She was meant to bear children. She was not the right class for a doctor's wife, of course, but she was quiet; she would never obtrude.

It was at this time that Edward made a strange remark: "If Mrs. Pritchard should die before I do, and you are still alive, Mary, I would marry you."

What could Mary M'Leod say to such strange words? She could only marvel and worship; but she would treasure those words through the painful experience to come.

It would have seemed to her that her lover was more than a man; he was a god.

*   *   *

It may have been that Mary Jane was aware of her servant's condition. She herself had suffered many pregnancies, and it is possible that Mary M'Leod betrayed her state in some way. She was the motherly type and, had the child been legitimately conceived, there is no doubt that she would have been in a state of ecstasy at the prospect of bearing it. But even though she knew she was not to bear the child, there may have been something in her demeanour to betray her to Mary Jane.

And what would Mary Jane think after having discovered the girl and Edward kissing in a bedroom?

Then Mary M'Leod became ill and Edward prescribed for her a few days' rest. Mary Jane had had miscarriages herself, so it is almost certain that she was aware of what ailed Mary M'Leod.

But very quickly the girl had recovered and was about her duties once more. She was strong and healthy and in a few months had cast off all effects of the trouble.

But Edward would have been uneasy. He would have caught Mary Jane's gaze when she did not think he was aware of her. Mary Jane must have been beginning to think that she knew very little about the man she had married.

*   *   *

Edward thought continually of his debts. They were increasing, for the two medical students had to be fed and the profit they brought was not large. He had two banking accounts—one with the Clydesdale and the other with the City of Glasgow Banks—and they were both overdrawn. He would consider his debt to Mrs. Taylor and would surely wonder whether the old lady would have noticed a certain brooding quality about her daughter and question its meaning. What if the old woman prevailed on her daughter to burst out with her suspicions about her husband and the servant girl? What if she told of the kissing in the bedroom and the mysterious illness which Mary had suffered?

He became irritated every time he looked at Mary Jane. He began to think with increasing excitement how different the house would be without Mary Jane.

It was not that he urgently desired to make Mary M'Leod his wife. Mary was his willing mistress and he had to admit that there was—and always would be for him—an added enjoyment where there was an element of danger.

It is said that there was no motive for Pritchard's behaviour. Why should he have attempted to rid himself of Mary Jane? She was docile; Mary M'Leod was already his mistress; and he would gain nothing financially from Mary Jane's death.

But there must have been a motive; and I think the way to find it is to look to this strange man's character and to try to understand the thoughts which obsessed him as he walked through Kelvingrove or Queen's Park or down the main streets and little by-ways of his city. Not far from the house in Sauchiehall Street was Blythswood Square, where seven or eight years before a young woman had lived who had been suspected of murder. In those days people had talked of little else in Glasgow. The girl's father had arranged a good marriage for her, but a lover from the past had tried to blackmail her; that lover had drunk a cup of chocolate and died. And the girl, whose name was Madeleine Smith, had stood on trial for murder. The verdict had been 'Not Proven', though there had been many in Glasgow to believe her guilty.

Yet that girl had faced them all—police, prosecution and judge; she had pitted her wits against them and won, so that the jury had been forced to declare her guilt 'not proven'. And that was a young and inexperienced girl!

He was a doctor! If he wanted to kill anybody, would he have put arsenic in a cup of chocolate?

The very idea would make him laugh. He was a doctor, and the uses of drugs were known to him. Yet a *girl* had outwitted them. There was food for thought in that fact.

And Mary Jane? She angered him; she infuriated him. Not because as his wife she prevented his marrying Mary M'Leod; not because her death would make him rich. No one could point to him and say: "You had a motive for killing your wife!" as they could say to Madeleine Smith: "You wanted your ex-lover out of the way." How could they know of that over-whelming vanity, that dignity, that inability to see that the life of anyone else could conceivably be as important as his own?

Cesare Borgia had murdered men because he did not like the way they looked when they spoke his name. He poisoned them merely because they had witnessed slights he had received when he travelled in France. Cesare did not gain much from their deaths, but they died nevertheless. The Marquise de Brinvilliers lightly tried out her poisons on people whom she had never seen before she visited their sick beds in the Hôtel Dieu. She killed as Cesare killed, as housewives kill moths that may get into the wardrobe, as they set traps for mice in the pantry.

The dignity of Edward was wounded every time his wife looked at him, because he was aware she knew in her heart that Mary M'Leod had had a miscarriage; and because she had seen Edward kissing the girl in one of the bedrooms, she suspected that he was responsible for Mary's condition. It may have seemed to him that, when he caught Mary Jane's reproach-ful eyes upon him, he was forced to look away from that charming, dignified picture which he had made of himself and saw instead the true one—that of the man who had found it necessary to leave Hunmanby because of an unsavoury incident with a patient which, but for almost incredible luck, might have obliged him to retire from practice; he saw the picture of the man who was in debt to her parents; perhaps he saw the murderer of Elizabeth M'Girn; certainly he saw the man who had been kissing the servant for whom he had arranged an abortion.

All this may seem no great inducement to commit murder, but Edward was a murderer of the calibre of Cesare Borgia and Marie de Brinvilliers. He shared in common with them the opinion that anyone who contributed to his discomfort should be removed, because *he* was all-important and they were quite insignificant.

This is the bond between these murderers. They were without conscience because they were unable to imagine themselves in any other person's place. They could look at suffering without its occurring to them to think: Suppose that had been happening to me. They could not put themselves into another person's place because, to them, that would have been like a giant trying to get into the skin of a dwarf.

All the same, the removal of Mary Jane could not be as easily accomplished as that of Elizabeth M'Girn. Elizabeth had been alive and well, full of health and vitality, one hour, and dead the next. Mary Jane must be dealt with in another way.

Did he remember that cold feeling of terror which the insurance people had aroused within him? With Mary Jane who was his wife, he would have to go very cautiously.

*   *   *

In the October which followed the summer of Mary M'Leod's abortion, Mary Jane began to have bouts of illness. She lost her appetite and was very sick; then she would recover a little, but after each bout she seemed to lose weight and be unable to regain it.

As the members of the family would doubtless notice this, it may have been that one of the children wrote to Fanny, the eldest girl who was with the Taylors in Edinburgh (since Edward's financial difficulties Fanny more or less lived with her grandparents at No. 1 Lauder Road, Edinburgh) and on hearing that her daughter had been unwell, Mrs. Taylor as usual suggested that a little of her native air would do her good.

Mary Jane went to Edinburgh for three weeks and there she very quickly regained her health, which was no doubt attributed by the Taylors to the superior Edinburgh air and the fact that poor Mary Jane was relieved of her domestic duties.

While she was away, Edward made several purchases. One day in November he bought an ounce of tartarized antimony, and a few days later an ounce of tincture of aconite.

News came from Edinburgh that Mary Jane was improving; in fact she was almost well again. Mrs. Taylor wanted to keep dear Mary Jane with her; she believed that under her care her daughter would soon be well again.

What were Edward's thoughts as he waited for Mary Jane's return? Was he anxious? Did he wonder whether he had been wise in agreeing to Mary Jane's visit to her parents? What were they going to say when she returned home and found that the attacks had begun again?

The two medical students were over-zealous and showing too much interest. They were regarding Mary Jane as a 'case', and one day they engaged Edward in conversation about his wife's illness; they said they thought it must be an unusual one. Edward told them coldly that it was not beyond *his* comprehension. They asked for a diagnosis, like good pupils of the master. He hesitated briefly, then told them it was gastric fever.

But they disturbed him, those two. They knew a little, but a little in some circumstances could be too much.

Knowing what we know of Edward's character from the impression he made on those about him, from letters, from his lectures, we can speculate on his reasoning during that time.

Mary Jane must die; he had made up his mind to that. It was a pity he could not give her the pleasant easy death which he had given Elizabeth M'Girn. Poor Mary Jane! She deserved to die easily.

But it was impossible, of course. A murderer dare not repeat himself—at least not in the nineteenth century. Mary Jane's death must be a slow one. The Taylors must see her growing weaker and weaker; they must be prepared for her death. If they were not, he would have that fiery Mrs. Taylor demanding to know what he had done to her dear Mary Jane, and stirring up trouble probably.

He knew how she would die. She would die slowly, by carefully administered doses of antimony; but antimony, being a mineral poison, left traces in the body after death, so there must be no unpleasant enquiry after poor Mary Jane's departure. As a doctor he believed he could arrange that.

He had chosen a poison which could be given in the easiest way. In the form of tartar emetic it could be administered without detection. It was true that the effects of the poison were agonizing but—poor Mary Jane—it was the only way. By using tartar emetic he could regulate the dose; he could make her very ill indeed or only slightly ill; he could discontinue the dose for a few days and she would recover a little.

There could not be a better way of assuring her family that she was suffering from a recurring illness, if she recovered a little but grew weaker after every bout.

How could he have contemplated his wife's suffering, as he did? Surely only the most cruel person could do this.

Edward Pritchard was a strange man. I have no doubt that

he made satisfactory excuses to himself. He was the complete hypocrite, and it may have been that he played his part so well because he could make himself believe what he wanted to.

I imagine that while he was planning this terrible and agonizing end for a wife who had done everything she possibly could to make a good home for him and his children, he made excuses for what he was doing to such an extent that he would feel it to be an act of benevolence.

He would look at Mary M'Leod with the children and tell himself that while they had Mary they would never lack a mother. The little ones clung to Mary, and now that Mary Jane was ill it was Mary M'Leod who was a mother to them. Children's loyalties changed quickly. They would soon forget their own mother in the new one he would provide for them ... if he should marry little Mary M'Leod.

It would be a terrible thing if the children were to discover him with Mary M'Leod, as their mother had done. He would do a great deal to prevent that.

And Mary M'Leod herself—here she was, living a life of sin in this house. That was really due to the existence of Mary Jane.

His reasoning may sound ridiculous, but he *was* ridiculous because he made daydreams and lived them. The affair of the walking stick, which he had had engraved with the inscription, reputed to have been given to him by Garibaldi is evidence of this. Putting his photographs up for sale in a shop window is similar evidence. Vanity to such a degree is like a narcotic toxin, and Pritchard's vanity could be likened to the Mexican cactus, peyotl, which transforms the world into a place of great beauty with colours such as are never seen on Earth and cannot even be imagined by people who are not under the influence of this drug; the return to reality after taking such drugs is painful, as painful as the return to reality would be for Pritchard when forced to see himself, not in his own vain image, but as he was in truth.

He must have grown very nervous while Mary Jane was in Edinburgh; every time those reports came of her improving health he must have realized the folly of letting her go. He must have felt angry with her meddlesome mother who was now crowing about Edinburgh air and implying that *she* knew how to cure poor Mary Jane.

He must have thought, too, of the students who had shown interest. It was disconcerting to have them in the house, prying; they would, unfortunately, consider it their duty to pry. Were they not there to learn?

He was worried about the servant, Catherine Lattimer.

Middle-aged women were notoriously inquisitive. Had she known what had ailed young Mary M'Leod a few months ago? How could he be sure? Perhaps he felt uncomfortable having her in the house.

However, he decided to get rid of Catherine Lattimer. He did not want her talking. He watched her and noticed that she had a friend who came to see her often, and one day when the friend was with her, he stealthily went down to the basement where he found Catherine entertaining.

After the friend had gone, he called Catherine to him and gave her three months' notice. She was to leave at Candlemas— the 2nd February.

Catherine Lattimer accepted her notice with a good grace. She had been caught entertaining her friend with food from the Pritchard larder; it seemed a good reason. Perhaps, too, she thought that there was a great deal to do in a house where the mistress was so often ailing and there was such a lot of running up and down stairs.

*　　　*　　　*

Mary Jane returned, and when she had been home a few weeks the attacks began again.

These attacks were having a terrible effect on Mary Jane's mind as well as on her body. There would have been occasions when she found it difficult to catch at her thoughts. Ideas would come into her head—vague ideas which she could not quite understand.

It must have happened that, as she lay in her bed after the violence of the pain had subsided, exhausted in mind and body, deeply under the depressing influence of antimony, hideous doubts came to her. Mary Jane had been brought up as a cherished child, sheltered from anything that was in the least unpleasant. It had been her habit to turn away when told to turn away, to discuss nothing improper. Now her poor dazed mind reacted in the old way; the habit had been formed, and Mary Jane, sick and exhausted, very close to death, could not face the doubt which had come into her mind.

But as she lay there did she think of the fire at Berkeley Terrace? Did she think of the flaunting girl who had at times shown a faint trace of insolence in her manner, even towards Edward? Did she remember having seen Edward kissing Mary M'Leod, and the girl's sudden illness during which Edward had attended her? Did it occur to her that these terrifying attacks came to her after meals or drinking a glass of wine? And how often did Edward himself bring that glass of wine to her with a "Drink this, my love. It will put some life into you"? Did she sometimes detect a strange flavour? Edward might say: "It's your taste, my dear. Drink it up. It's just what you need", but—and there was the doubt which it was so hard to face—could she trust Edward?

Did she think to herself: "I am afraid of Edward. What is Edward doing to me?" And then did she try to push the thought away, or refuse to listen to that faint note of warning from within her mind?

It was unpleasant and improper to believe your husband could want to murder you. Therefore Mary Jane must not entertain such thoughts.

She knew that Edward had dismissed Catherine Lattimer. Catherine was a kindly woman who had been a great help in the sick room. If Catherine went, she—Mary Jane—would be in this house with only the children, Edward and Mary M'Leod.

She asked Catherine when she would be leaving and Catherine told her she was going on the next day.

Then suddenly Mary Jane was seized with panic; she clung to Catherine's hands and managed to beg her not to leave her, but to stay with her.

Edward, coming into the room heard what she said. He would have looked at that cool-eyed woman of sound sense, the woman whom he had dismissed, not because she was giving a friend food in the kitchen, but because he wanted her out of the house.

He acted quickly. This woman Lattimer must suspect nothing. The new servant was to arrive on the 16th. This was the 1st February. He asked Catherine humbly, and with sincerity shining from his eyes, whether she would consider staying on with them until the new woman came.

Catherine agreed to do so.

Edward must have been quite panic-stricken himself then, for it would have occurred to him that, in Mary Jane's drug-fuddled mind there was a suspicion that he was trying to poison her.

*   *   *

Edward acted boldly. He could not know what Mary Jane had said to Catherine Lattimer; therefore he decided on a prompt action which must allay all suspicion.

He would call in another opinion. Only thus could he eradicate that dangerous thought from Mary Jane's mind; only thus could he divert any suspicion which may have entered that of Catherine Lattimer.

He thought of Dr. James Moffat Cowan, who was a retired doctor and a second cousin of Mary Jane's. He was living in Edinburgh, and, if he wrote to him that day, he could tell Catherine Lattimer that he had written; he could tell Mary Jane that he had written; the letter would take a little time to reach Dr. Cowan, and during that time he, Edward, would use all his skill in getting Mary Jane to rally. The human body, even such a tortured one as Mary Jane's, was wonderfully resilient; and he had been careful with his doses—never enough to be fatal, only just enough to produce the symptoms of gastric illness of which eventually Mary Jane must die.

Moreover, Dr. Cowan was not young, and Edward probably felt that it would be easier to deceive an older man than one who had knowledge of more modern discoveries.

The letter he wrote to Dr. Cowan declared his extreme anxiety on account of his wife; he told of her alarming attacks which resulted in a cramping of the limbs; he felt that, in such circumstances, the only wise thing to do was to call in another opinion.

Dr. Cowan arrived on the 7th February, a few days after Edward had written to him. Mary Jane had been feeling very much better during the last few days; she had had one or two attacks but they had been very slight; Edward had not been so foolish as to let them stop altogether; and Mary Jane was growing optimistic about her condition.

If she remembered that terrible fear which had come to her in her dazed condition it is likely that she would have dismissed it as a madness. Edward—poison her! She would think that that was the sort of thing which might happen to other people, but not in respectable families like theirs. And had not Edward allowed—no, begged—Catherine Lattimer to stay? And had he not asked dear James Cowan to come and have a look at her? Because, Edward would have explained, he was worried about her; and it was always advisable for a doctor to have a second opinion about a case which worried him; this one happened to worry him very much indeed because the patient was a very precious person to Edward.

This is the smooth and hypocritical style in his diary and letters. It is certain that he would have used it in full force at that time with Mary Jane.

One imagines the poor woman's shame throughout those days; it might even have raised her spirits, have given her an extra impetus to regain her health.

When Dr. Cowan arrived at the house in Sauchiehall Street, Edward was waiting for him. Gravely he talked to him about

Mary Jane's case, stressing his fears; he was determined to prepare Dr. Cowan to find Mary Jane less ill than he, Edward, described her; it might have been that he thought that thus Dr. Cowan would dismiss a great deal of Edward's anxiety as the natural feeling of a husband for a wife, rather than a doctor for a patient. It might have been that he thought Dr. Cowan would go back to Edinburgh and tell them there: "Oh yes, Mary Jane is certainly far from well, but perhaps Edward worries a little unduly. One cannot expect poor Edward to see Mary Jane as an ordinary patient."

With the help of Mary M'Leod, Mary Jane was able to dress, and she came down to the drawing-room to greet her second cousin.

Edward must have been delighted to see that his stratagem had worked, for Dr. Cowan was actually more inclined to make light of Mary Jane's illness than he would have done if he had not been prepared for something far worse.

He asked Mary Jane how she felt; she told him about her inability to retain food, and the cramp of her limbs after the attacks, of the dazed condition which seized her. Dr. Cowan scolded her for getting up on his account, and told her that he thought she should go back to bed.

When she had gone, Mary M'Leod helping her, the doctors talked together. Dr. Cowan prescribed mustard poultices to be applied to her stomach; and since she could not retain her food, he thought a little iced champagne would revive her. He accepted Edward's diagnosis that Mary Jane's ailment was a form of irritation of the stomach.

Edward must have congratulated himself on the clever move of calling in Dr. Cowan. Who but a man such as himself, a man surely possessed of superhuman qualities, would have dared act so boldly when he was in the process of poisoning his wife? Why, that very day, he had bought more tartarized antimony and tincture of aconite.

Dr. Cowan had planned to stay the night in Glasgow and return to Edinburgh the following day. As soon as he had left, so Edward planned, Mary Jane should have another attack, a violent one to make up for the few days' respite.

But even while he must have been congratulating himself, Dr. Cowan delivered the blow.

It was a big house, said Dr. Cowan; there were the children to be looked after in addition to all the work which must attach itself to a doctor's household. He knew what that could mean. And there were only two maids—that young girl and the elderly woman who, he understood, was under notice. There was a new woman coming on the 16th, Edward assured him; they managed very well. The children were very good. No one need feel uneasy about them on that score.

But he was uneasy, Dr. Cowan persisted And he could see that Mary Jane was anxious also. It was natural. She was a house-proud woman. He had an idea. He was going to ask Mrs. Taylor to come and look after Mary Jane; that would take a great burden from the servants and a weight off Edward's mind, he was sure.

Edward must have been furious. The idea of having that inquisitive old woman in the house was alarming.

He protested that it was not fair to Mrs. Taylor. She was not as young as she had been. She had her own house in Lauder Road. No, Edward would *not* impose this extra burden on her.

Dr. Cowan would have laughed at that and assured Edward that he would be unable to do anything *but* accept the help of his mother-in-law; he had had strict orders to report to Mrs. Taylor on her daughter's health and, when she heard what he had to tell her, he, Dr. Cowan, was sure that not many days would elapse before Mrs. Taylor arrived to look after her dear Mary Jane.

Then Edward surely cursed himself for letting this man into the house. He saw complications if the old lady came. He would not have her upsetting his plans. She would want to cook for Mary Jane, and she would have her nose in everything.

But he quickly realized that there was one thing more dangerous than having Mrs. Taylor in the house, and that would be to make any attempt to prevent her coming. The old Edward stirred himself. Why should he, Edward Pritchard, who had managed so successfully in Hunmanby and Berkeley Terrace, be afraid of the old woman?

The more he thought of her being in the house, the less he feared her. He may even have begun to find some pleasure in the thought of carrying on with his evil work right beneath that inquisitive old nose.

*   *   *

The night Dr. Cowan left Glasgow, Mary Jane was taken very ill again. Edward had given her chloroform and the iced champagne which had been prescribed by Dr. Cowan.

Mary Jane awoke during the night to find that the terrible pain was with her; and with it came the cramp in her limbs and the horrible fear in her mind. She screamed in her agony. Edward got up and called Catherine Lattimer and Mary M'Leod into the bedroom.

It may have been the sight of the doctor and Mary together which brought back Mary Jane's fears. She must have been suddenly terrified of this house and the man who, she sensed, wanted to be rid of her. She may have remembered that Dr. Cowan had gone and that he had taken with him her chance of getting into touch with the safe world of Edinburgh.

She must have been thinking of her mother, who had told her that one of the doctors who had qualified with Michael Taylor was in practice in Glasgow. His name was Dr. Gairdner.

It is heartrending to contemplate the distress which must have been Mary Jane's as she lay there. That fear, which she had dismissed as unworthy and shameful, would have come back in full force. Why had she begun to recover before Dr. Cowan came? Why had she been taken so ill immediately after he had left?

She *must* see Dr. Gairdner.

She looked to Catherine whom she would have felt to be her only ally, Catherine, who was under notice to leave her alone in this frightening house.

She declared then that she wanted to see Dr. Gairdner. She demanded that he be brought to her.

Edward would certainly have felt more than a twinge of alarm. It was one thing to call in Dr. Cowan when there had been two or three days to prepare for his coming; it was quite another to have a young doctor called in while Mary Jane was actually under the influence of poison.

But what could he do? Refuse her request? If only Catherine Lattimer had gone when she was supposed to have gone, there would have been no need to feel that anxiety. Catherine's eyes would be upon him, and he told her rather sadly that since his wife wished to see Dr. Gairdner, he must be sent for. Mary M'Leod should go at once and fetch him. Mary obeyed.

Mary Jane lay back on her bed, her hands contorted with extraordinary spasms. Edward uneasily watched while Catherine rubbed those hands. He would be aware of Mary Jane's eyes on him and he would see in them not only terror but something he had not seen before: suspicion that he was responsible for her present state.

Within a short time Mary M'Leod returned with Dr. Gairdner. Mary Jane was capable of speech then. She reminded him that he had been a class-fellow of her brother Michael, and Dr. Gairdner replied that he remembered Michael Taylor well. Mary Jane then apologized for not calling him before. Gairdner looked at her oddly; her eyes were so wild and she did not appear to be able to control her voice or her thoughts;

his eyes rested on her hands which lay on the coverlet; the wrists were turned in, and the thumbs inverted towards the wrists.

Mary Jane was looking at her husband, who was watching her sorrowfully, and suddenly she cried out: "If you cry you are a hypocrite."

There was silence in the room, and this must have been the most alarming moment Edward had encountered since he had begun to work for Mary Jane's destruction. He must have felt that he needed all his wits to extricate himself from this awkward position, and that Gairdner was going to think something very strange was taking place in this house; he would have been terrified of what Mary Jane was going to say next.

But immediately that picture of himself—so important, clever beyond all men—came to his mind. Who was this Gairdner? A class-fellow of Michael Taylor's! Edward had the utmost contempt for him. How could such a pigmy interfere with the schemes of mighty Edward Pritchard!

Dr. Gairdner had turned to the fire to warm his hands before beginning the examination. Seeing him turn away and, no doubt, not realizing that he had merely gone to the fire, Mary Jane screamed out as loudly as she could: "Oh, you cruel, cruel man, you unfeeling man! Don't leave me."

Edward would surely have been terrified in that moment. He must have realized that for the first time Mary Jane had escaped from his domination. She knew that he was trying to kill her and she was ready to expose him to Gairdner.

Dr. Gairdner went quickly to the bed and said soothingly that he was not going to leave her; he was merely going to warm his hands by the fire.

There would have been a short whispered conversation while the doctors stood by the fire. Edward's hope was to make Gairdner believe that Mary Jane was intoxicated; he told him that he was uneasy about giving her champagne, but that had been prescribed by Dr. Cowan. Gairdner said he thought champagne most unsuitable in view of Mrs. Pritchard's hysterical condition; and Edward had the satisfaction of knowing that when Gairdner returned to the bed he was prepared to accept any wild statements, made by Mary Jane, as the ravings of a woman drunk on champagne.

Mary Jane's poor mind sought to take advantage of Gairdner's presence to call for help. But the poison had deeply affected her mind as well as her body, and she would have found it difficult to collect her thoughts. She would only know fear . . . terrible fear . . . and feel that the only two whom she might trust were Gairdner and Catherine Lattimer.

"You are hypocrites . . ." she moaned. "You are all hypo-crites. . . ." She could find nothing else to say.

Gairdner was puzzled, Edward noticed with pleasure. Gairdner was young, and it was not often that a doctor was called upon to witness the results of poisoning by tartar emetic.

Gairdner was loth to confess his perplexity. He recom-mended an immediate cessation of intoxicants and suggested a light diet instead. He admitted that he could not understand the spasms in the hands. Edward slyly asked him if he thought Mrs. Pritchard was suffering from catalepsy.

Very little was known about catalepsy at this time, and Edward would have looked knowledgeable when he made this suggestion. It would have been difficult for Gairdner to admit ignorance, Edward guessed. No young doctor liked to do that. No doubt Edward told himself then that he had been foolish to worry about Gairdner. All the world were fools; only he was wise. As if anyone could successfully interfere with his plans!

Gairdner said he would call again the next day.

That was satisfactory from Edward's point of view; he and the patient would be prepared.

Mary Jane was very much better the next day when Dr. Gairdner called. It seemed to her that what had happened the previous night was a bad dream. She had suffered from hallucinations; terrible thoughts had come to her, thoughts which she could not quite catch, and they had disturbed her.

She even felt she could eat; she had a lightly boiled egg and a little milk. Nothing happened—no sickness, no pain; she felt a great deal better. When Dr. Gairdner saw her he was pleased, for he believed he had worked the miracle. What she needed was good plain food. Obviously she was suffering from a weak digestion in the first place, and that old fool Cowan with his champagne and chloroform had aggravated that. What could one expect from an old man with antiquated ideas!

Edward was charming to him, telling him that he had put his finger on exactly what was wrong. He thought Mary Jane was certainly improving and there would not be any need to call in Gairdner again. Gairdner also thought this would not be necessary.

Edward congratulated himself, but was not so pleased when he learned that Gairdner had written to Michael Taylor telling him that he was not satisfied with his sister's condition and he thought it would be an excellent idea if she could go and stay with her brother for a while. Michael wrote to Edward saying that he would be delighted if Mary Jane came to stay with him. He had heard how ill she was from Gairdner, and would be pleased to look after her. Edward's reply was that, for the time being, Mary Jane was not fit to travel. When she was a little better he would be delighted to take advantage of Michael's kindness.

Clearly Edward must have been perturbed by all this, and decided that there must be no further delay.

The next day Mrs. Taylor arrived.

*　　　*　　　*

How happy Mary Jane must have been to have her mother in the house! All her fears must have left her, for how could she believe that evil could come near her when her mother was there to protect her? It was like being a child again. But Edward would have realized that the old lady was a more formidable menace than either Cowan or Gairdner. They were clever men and Mrs. Taylor was merely a woman; but Mrs. Taylor was Mary Jane's own mother, and she would be like a tigress whose cub is in danger. He knew that he would have to exercise great caution with Mrs. Taylor under his roof.

There had been one or two outbursts of sickness in the house. Connell, one of the medical students, and one of the children had suffered from attacks like those of Mary Jane. They must have eaten something intended for Mrs. Pritchard. It could so easily happen. They began to wonder whether there was something contagious or infectious in Mrs. Pritchard's illness; which was all to the good from Edward's point of view.

Mrs. Taylor was very respectful to Edward, so it was clear to him that Mary Jane had said nothing to her mother that was anything like that strange outburst of hers before Gairdner. He began to believe that Mary Jane really had been intoxicated by the champagne.

All was going better than he dared hope, when there occurred the affair of the tapioca.

Mary Jane's appetite was returning, for Mrs. Taylor was insisting on cooking most of her daughter's food. Mary Jane liked the way *she* cooked; she was sure *she* could tempt Mary Jane.

Then one day Mary Jane asked for tapioca pudding.

Mrs. Taylor came down to the hall and sent one of the children out to buy some tapioca; and seeing Edward there, she told him of Mary Jane's fancy and asked if he thought it could do her any harm. None at all, said Edward. It would do her much good.

When the child brought the tapioca back to the house he was told to leave it on the lobby table until it was required. This he did. Edward must have found it there when he returned from his rounds. It would not take long to slip into his room with it, that room in which he kept his drugs, and with it mix a little tartar emetic, so that when Mary M'Leod, at the bidding of Catherine Lattimer, came to get the tapioca, it would not be noticed that the package had been tampered with.

When the pudding was ready, Mary M'Leod took it to the sick-room, but by this time Mary Jane's appetite must have failed her, for she did not want it. It seemed a pity to waste it, thought Mrs. Taylor; and she herself ate it.

It was very shortly after that when Mrs. Taylor began to suffer violent pains. She felt that the tapioca had disagreed with her, but how could that be? It never had before and it was such a simple food.

Later she was very ill.

* * *

Mrs. Taylor was no fool, and I believe that she would have said to herself that if a simple tapioca pudding was responsible for making a woman as ill as she had been there must have been something wrong with it and more in that pudding than the usual ingredients.

She would have been very worried, unable to sleep easily; and her headaches would not be improved by her anxieties. She would need her Battley's Sedative Solution more than ever. This Solution was sold in chemists' shops of the day and contained a proportion of opium. Mrs. Taylor had been drinking this Solution for years so that she was able to take far larger doses than most people would.

I do not believe that, in the circumstances, she would be able to keep her fears to herself. The pudding intended for Mary Jane had been eaten by herself and she had suffered symptoms similar to those endured by Mary Jane. The inference must have been obvious. Someone in the house was tampering with Mary Jane's food. Obviously she could not discuss such a thing with Mary Jane in her present weak state. I think she may have confided in Edward. Her thoughts may have turned to Catherine Lattimer who was under notice. A flimsy reason for trying to poison the mistress of the house, but some women were vindictive. And who else could Mrs. Taylor suspect? Certainly not Edward.

If she did confide in Edward he must have decided immediately that Mrs. Taylor must die, and die quickly.

Edward would, of course, be smoothly silky, full of concern, very tender towards his mother-in-law as he could be in his most deadly moments. Mrs. Taylor would surely have told him that she intended to cook everything Mary Jane ate in future.

Poor blind Mrs. Taylor. If this is what happened, she had signed her own death warrant.

* * *

Catherine Lattimer left and the new servant, Mary Patterson, arrived to take her place.

Edward was wary of middle-aged women, and he was determined that this one should not see too much. He told Mary Patterson that she was not to go to the sick-room, because his wife was very ill and anything different from usual might upset her.

Edward must have been deeply disturbed. He would remember Mary Jane's outburst to Dr. Gairdner; after the affair of the tapioca Mrs. Taylor must be suspicious and if she and Mary Jane compared their suspicions, who could say how long it would be before they arrived at the right solution?

A few days later Mrs. Taylor gave Mary M'Leod a bottle and told her to go to the chemist and get it filled with Battley's Solution. Edward saw Mary on her way out and asked where she was going. How his eyes must have glistened when they rested on the bottle in Mary's hands! He probably thought that Mrs. Taylor's fancy for Battley's Sedative Solution gave him a good opportunity.

* * *

It was the 24th February and Mrs. Taylor had been in the house exactly two weeks. Edward saw his patients, and when the last had gone, rang for Mary M'Leod.

There would probably have been an added spice to love-making with Mary, now that Mrs. Taylor was in the house.

As he took her into a fumbling embrace there were steps outside the door and he heard Mrs. Taylor's voice calling. Mary's clothing had become disarranged and, as in a second Mrs. Taylor would be in the room, there seemed only one thing to do; he opened a cupboard door and pushed Mary inside, but not before the outer door had opened and Mrs. Taylor stood there looking at him.

It was perfectly clear to Mrs. Taylor what had happened. She had interrupted Edward while he was philandering with the servant girl. She would know in that instant that Edward was not the man she had believed him to be; there were strange things going on in this house, and if she could discover him guilty of one thing, might he not be of another?

She declared that she was shocked beyond measure and that Mary M'Leod should be sent away. Then she left him.

When he let Mary out of the cupboard he would not let her see that he was worried. He would tell her to deny everything if Mrs. Taylor questioned her, but he did not intend that Mrs. Taylor should have much time for questioning.

She had but to link the tapioca incident with this one and she might suddenly grasp the truth of what was happening in this house.

He knew he had to act quickly. He did not think Mrs. Taylor would talk of her discovery to Mary Jane at present, for Mary Jane was not strong enough for such shocks. But later she would insist on taking Mary Jane away from the house; and that would of course ruin all his schemes.

He went into the lobby and, as though Providence had arranged it, he saw her coat hanging there. Often he would have seen her slip a certain bottle into the big pocket. If the bottle were there now, it would be simple.

The bottle was there. He took it and quickly carried it into his room.

*   *   *

Mary M'Leod had been sent to buy sausages for Mrs. Taylor's supper. Soon after she had given them to Mary Patterson to cook she heard a violent ringing of the bell in Mrs. Pritchard's room. Mrs. Taylor had shared the room with her daughter ever since her arrival, the doctor occupying the spare room.

When Mary entered the room she found that Mrs. Pritchard was sitting up in bed and that Mrs. Taylor was in a chair looking very ill; her face was a strange colour and her hands were hanging limply at her sides. She asked in a feeble voice for hot water.

Mary fetched the hot water, which Mrs. Taylor drank; then she sent Mary for more, but before Mary could bring it the bell began to clang again. Mary rushed back. Mrs. Taylor appeared to be unconscious, and Mrs. Pritchard, frantic with anxiety, told Mary to go at once and bring the doctor.

Edward was with a patient, but as soon as he was free he hurried upstairs to the sick room.

He took one look at Mrs. Taylor and sent Mary for a local doctor, James Paterson.

Edward must certainly have had to steel himself for the ordeal to come.

*   *   *

He met Dr. Paterson in the lobby, took him to the consulting room and told him that his mother-in-law had been writing a letter when she had suddenly collapsed, falling from her chair to the floor; she had been carried upstairs, he added. This happened, he went on, about an hour and a half ago; and Mrs. Taylor and Mrs. Pritchard had taken some bitter beer which had made them both sick.

Dr. Paterson replied that he was surprised that beer should have that effect, and thought it must have been something different.

Edward then told the deliberately unkind lie that his mother-in-law was in the habit of 'taking a drop too much to drink' at times. He then informed Paterson that his wife had been suffering from gastric fever and that Mrs. Taylor had come to nurse her.

It must have been an extraordinary sight which met Dr. Paterson's eyes when he entered the sick room. Mrs. Taylor was lying on the bed with her clothes on, and her little cap, in which was an artificial flower, had slipped to one side of her head. She appeared to be the victim of a sudden seizure. Mrs. Pritchard was in the bed, wearing a night-dress; her hair was wild and she was obviously frantic with anxiety.

Paterson, examining the old lady, did not think she had the look of one who partook often and freely of intoxicants. She was pale, her lips were livid, her breathing slow and very laborious, the pulse almost imperceptible, the skin clammy; and on lifting her eyelids he found her pupils contracted.

Paterson felt sure that she was under the influence of opium or some other strong narcotic. He felt sure that she was dying.

Edward drew him away from the bed and they talked in whispers in a corner of the room. Paterson said he thought there was nothing they could do. The old lady was past help.

Edward turned to the bed, smiled at Mary Jane, and laid his hand on Mrs. Taylor's shoulder. "You are getting better, darling," he said; but Paterson shook his head and muttered: "Never, in this world."

Paterson's attention was then caught by the other occupant of the bed. Indeed, feeling the old lady to be past help, it was the younger woman who held his attention. He noticed the peculiar flush on her cheeks, and her high-pitched voice; she seemed as though she were on the verge of collapse. She was clearly very disturbed by her mother's condition, and Pritchard had told him that she was recovering from an attack of gastric fever. But there was more than that, thought Paterson. He could almost believe that depression of manner was a symptom of poisoning.

He might have diagnosed cholera; but it was not cholera, of course. Gastric fever! Certainly it was not gastric fever!

Poisoning? Surely what he saw might be the depressing effects of antimony!

Dr. Paterson was a man who believed that the etiquette of the medical profession should never be broken in any circumstance. He had been called in to see Mrs. Taylor. His opinion of Mrs. Pritchard had not been asked. But poison!

Edward, who would have been watching him closely, would have lost no time in conducting him from the sick-room. He could see that Paterson was puzzled and apprehensive, but Edward thought that it was due to Mrs. Taylor.

He explained that Mrs. Taylor was in the habit of taking Battley's Sedative Solution, and that only a short while ago she had sent the maid out to get a half-pound bottle refilled. It was his opinion, said Edward, that Mrs. Taylor had exceeded the dose. She must in fact have had a 'good swig' at it.

He said if anything further happened, he would send for Paterson, who replied that there was nothing he could do. Paterson did not like the house; he did not like being called in to an old lady who had clearly been quite healthy and who had come under the influence of acute narcotism. What he liked still less was the thought of the woman in the bed. What if he were right about her? What if she *were* under the depressing influence of antimony? Who in this house would know how to administer the doses? Who would be able to procure them with the utmost ease?

It was a sinister house, Dr. Paterson concluded on that February night, and he was a man who liked his life to run along smooth lines. He did not want to hear any more about it.

*   *   *

But he did hear more. A few hours later Mary M'Leod was at his door. Would he come at once, for Mrs. Taylor was much worse? He sent a message by Mary M'Leod—his compliments to Dr. Pritchard, but as he was certain there was nothing he could do to save Mrs. Taylor's life, he did not propose getting up. If Pritchard really thought he could do any more than he himself could, and sent again for him, he would come; but they both knew it was hopeless.

Then Paterson once more tried to forget all about the house in which he had seen such strange things.

*   *   *

Mary Patterson and Jessie Nabb, an old woman who came in to do the washing, prepared Mrs. Taylor's body for her coffin. Mary Jane meanwhile had been moved to the spare room. She seemed in a daze of bewildered misery, which was probably less than it might otherwise have been because her mind was not very clear as to what was going on.

The two women found in the pocket of Mrs. Taylor's dress a bottle which was about three-quarters full of a brown liquid. On the bottle was the inscription, 'Two drops equal to three of laudanum'.

They uncorked the bottle and smelt it; they found the smell very similar to that of laudanum. Then Mary Patterson took it from Jessie Nabb and pushed it under the chest of drawers. But before they had finished preparing the body, Edward came in and asked for the bottle they had found in Mrs. Taylor's pocket. They gave it to him. Edward raised his eyebrows and looked very shocked. "Good Heavens!" he cried. "Has she taken this much since Tuesday?" Then he turned to the women and asked them to say nothing about the bottle, as it would not do for it to be known that someone in the house of a doctor in his position, took such stuff; and, adding that he would take the bottle to show Mrs. Pritchard, he went out.

* * *

Old Mr. Taylor was heartbroken when he received the wire telling him to come to Glasgow. He could not understand why or how it had happened. Mrs. Taylor had been so well when she had left Edinburgh. How could it have happened so suddenly? Edward explained that it was paralysis followed by apoplexy. He then suggested that Mr. Taylor should go to Dr. Paterson for the death certificate, as it was better that it should come from a doctor who was not a member of the family.

Mr. Taylor went along to Dr. Paterson, and Edward must have waited in some trepidation for his return.

The old man was quite bewildered when he came back. He had found Dr. Paterson very brusque and unco-operative. Moreover he had refused to give the certificate. He had said he was surprised that Dr. Pritchard should have sent to him for it when, as a medical practitioner, he should have known that the certificate was not to be given to friends of the deceased but to the District Registrar.

Edward was not unduly alarmed; he felt sure that, when approached by the District Registrar, Paterson would give a satisfactory certificate.

* * *

Mrs. Taylor's body was taken to Edinburgh; and the day before the funeral, Edward was walking in Sauchiehall Street when he came face to face with Dr. Paterson. He felt the need to ingratiate himself with the man, for he was hoping he was not going to be difficult about supplying Mrs. Taylor's death certificate. He hailed him as a friend, and spoke of the sad affair of Mrs. Taylor's death, explaining that the next day he was going to Edinburgh for the funeral. He was a little anxious about leaving his wife though, for she, of course, would not be well enough to accompany him to Edinburgh.

Edward did a daring thing. He was eager to win Paterson's confidence. Because he had never considered other people of enough importance to attempt to understand them, he believed that Paterson was a pale shadow of himself; therefore he appealed to Paterson's vanity. Nothing could make him feel more reconciled to going to Edinburgh than the thought that his wife was in the care of someone whom he could trust. Would Dr. Paterson call in and see Mrs. Pritchard while he was away?

Paterson wanted never to go near Pritchard's house again, but etiquette forbade him to say so, or to refuse to visit a patient when requested to do so.

When he called on Mrs. Pritchard on the following day he was able to study her more closely than when he had called on her mother. She told him about her symptoms—the sickness and the constant thirst; and he became more and more uneasy, for everything he discovered about her confirmed rather than dispelled the idea that she was being poisoned with antimony.

He was in a quandary. He was not the sort of man who cared to take risks. How could he say to a patient: "Someone in this house is trying to poison you"? How could he call on Pritchard and say: "I suspect you of attempting to poison your wife"?

He visualized unpleasantness, a court case and—horror of horrors—himself in the wrong. Perhaps there was some disease of which he knew nothing. He could be held up to ridicule; his patients would dwindle away. He imagined the whispers: "Don't call in Paterson. He'll accuse you of poisoning your wife!"

What could he do? He could only prescribe what he would prescribe for a person who he thought was being slowly poisoned by antimony.

He told Mrs. Pritchard to take champagne and brandy at intervals, and in very small quantities. That would strengthen her. She should take small pieces of ice occasionally to relieve the burning thirst. She needed foods such as beef tea, calves foot jelly, chicken soup—easily digested and nourishing. These should be taken in small quantities but frequently.

He left the house, feeling he had done all that a cautious man could do, and fervently he hoped that he would never hear of the Pritchards again.

He had decided that at least he would not sign the death

certificate for Mrs. Taylor; and accordingly he returned the schedule which the Registrar had sent him, with a note stating that the death of Mrs. Taylor was sudden, unexpected and to him mysterious.

Edward's luck was good once more. There occurred some confusion in the Registrar's office, and the note which accompanied the schedule was lost; and as the Registrar had heard that both Dr. Paterson and Dr. Pritchard had been in attendance on Mrs. Taylor, presuming that he had sent the form to the wrong doctor, he then sent another to Dr. Pritchard.

Edward stated that Mrs. Taylor had died of paralysis and apoplexy; and that, but for later events, would have ended the matter, and none but Dr. Paterson would ever have doubted that Mrs. Taylor's death had been due to natural causes.

*   *   *

With Mrs. Taylor safely out of the way, Edward felt ready to continue with his plans regarding Mary Jane. He had been surely upset by Paterson's refusal to give the death certificate but, with that peculiar blindness of his, he let himself believe that Paterson, that stickler for etiquette, had refused to do this because he had seen Mrs. Taylor only once—on the occasion of her death. He decided to placate Paterson by calling on him and telling him how grateful he was for his care of Mrs. Pritchard, and that since she had taken his advice her condition was considerably improved.

But he was determined that Mary Jane must be quickly disposed of. Her brother, Dr. Michael Taylor, was constantly writing to him asking about Mary Jane's health, and clearly the business should be finished with quickly.

Meanwhile he had continued to buy tartarized antimony and tincture of aconite—a little at a time; and about ten days after his return to Glasgow, while at table with the family, he cut a piece of cheese which he sent up to Mary Jane by Mary M'Leod. As one end of the cheese had been dipped into a solution of tartar emetic, it must have been risky having it put on the table and cutting off the poisoned piece while it was there. But Edward had the arrogance of a Borgia and the recklessness of Marie de Brinvilliers because he believed that it was fitting for him to deal death to any whom he wished to remove, as did those other two murderers.

When the cheese was taken up to Mary Jane she asked Mary M'Leod to taste it and tell her if it was ripe. The girl did so, taking a very small portion. She declared it to have a strange taste and said it made her mouth burn unpleasantly. The

cheese was therefore taken down to the kitchen, where Mary
Patterson ate a larger portion of it than Mary M'Leod had
done. The result was that Mary Patterson was violently ill and
had to stay in bed for a day or so.

*   *   *

A few nights later Edward asked Mary Patterson to make an
egg flip for Mrs. Pritchard, telling her he would get the sugar
for it. There was nothing unusual in this for the sugar was not
kept in the kitchen. He returned with two lumps which he put
in the glass. Mary Patterson tasted the mixture when she had
added the hot water and, making a wry face, mentioned to
Mary M'Leod that it had a very unpleasant taste. It was taken
to Mary Jane who, soon after, felt very ill. Meanwhile Mary
Patterson began to suffer from a return of that attack which she
had experienced after eating the cheese.

Naturally Edward heard of the illness and knew what was
happening. Mary Patterson was tasting food which was prepared for Mary Jane. Why? Was she a natural taster of this
and that? Or was she seeking to make some discovery? These
were questions which Edward must surely have asked himself.
He was clearly at this time growing uneasy.

*   *   *

It was a few days later when Mary Patterson heard Mrs.
Pritchard's bell ringing continually; no one answered it, so
she went to the consulting room where she knew the doctor to
be; for she had been told that Mary M'Leod, and no one else,
was to attend Mrs. Pritchard.

There was no answer when she knocked, so she opened the
door to find that she could only open it a little way, because
it seemed as though some heavy object had been put in front
of it or that someone was holding it to prevent its being opened.

She then started to go upstairs to Mrs. Pritchard's room, but
before she had got very far the door of the consulting room
opened and the doctor came out. Mary Patterson saw Mary
M'Leod slip out behind him.

Now Edward would realize the need for immediate action.
Mary Patterson was a woman of sound common sense; she had
tasted cheese and egg flip and had become ill; she knew that
the doctor and Mary M'Leod had been together in the consulting room and anxious that no one should burst in on them
suddenly. She would, of course, soon draw her own conclusions
as to the meaning of this if she had not done so already.

That night Mary Jane became delirious, and it was clear that
her condition had undergone a change. Edward sent for Dr.

Paterson. It was a desperate thing to do, but he had no notion of Paterson's suspicions; and in view of Mrs. Taylor's recent death and the fact that Mary Jane was his wife, it would be better this time to have another doctor in the case, if it should happen that he should be needed.

Paterson was horrified by the change in Mary Jane. There was a wild expression in her eyes, which were red and sunken; she was very flushed, her pulse weak and rapid. Although she was delirious she recognized him and, when he bent over her, caught at his hand as though appealing to him not to leave her; he was reminded vividly of his suspicions. Edward told him that she had scarcely slept for five days and nights, and Paterson prescribed a mixture consisting of thirty drops of solution of morphia, thirty drops of ipecacuanha wine, five or ten drops of chlorodyne and an ounce of cinnamon water, suggesting that this should be repeated in four hours if the first draught did not give relief.

Edward humbly agreed that Mary Jane should be given this and Paterson left.

Mary Jane's agonies were over. She died at one o'clock that morning.

* * *

Standing with Mary M'Leod and Mary Patterson at the death-bed, Edward gave an exhibition of husbandly grief, crying: "Come back, come back, my dear Mary Jane. Don't leave your dear Edward." He turned to the servants and bade them bring hot water and mustard poultices, declaring he refused to believe that his wife was dead.

Then he made an extraordinary remark. He cried: "What a brute! What a heathen! King has a rifle in his room. Go and get it and shoot me."

Was it possible that for a moment he felt remorse? Was he acting? Did he remember the terrible suffering he had inflicted on Mary Jane? Or was he trying to impress Mary Patterson? Was he wondering what was going on behind those cool eyes? Was he afraid that she was remembering the incidents of the cheese and the egg flip? He was not living in fifteenth-century Italy where life was cheap; he was not living in seventeenth-century France where it was held only slightly less cheap; he was in Scotland of the eighteen-sixties where life was precious and a murderer knew that an autopsy on his victim would certainly betray him.

Surely the times in which he was living had some effect on his character. He could not forget that in a civilized country murder was looked upon as a terrible crime. He had shown no remorse over Elizabeth M'Girn, nor over Mrs. Taylor. But Mary Jane was his wife and it might have been that temporarily he saw himself clearly as the callous murderer he was.

He recovered himself very quickly, and began to play the part of bereaved husband with exquisite skill.

He left Mary Patterson to wash the body of Mary Jane while he sent Mary M'Leod to tell Dr. Paterson that Mrs. Pritchard was dead, and there would be no need for him to come. He wrote some letters to Mary Jane's family and went out to post them. When he returned he sought out Mary Patterson—evidently he could not get the woman out of his mind—and told her that his wife had walked down the street with him and asked him to take care of their little girls.

After that display of feeling Edward no doubt felt that she now recognized him as a suitably bereaved and suffering husband.

*   *   *

When it was necessary to show his strength he would be the callous murderer who was prepared to deal death where he considered it necessary, and he cared not how cruel he was. Then he saw himself as clever, subtle, cunning, the man capable of committing the perfect crime. When he wished to see himself as the tender husband, he felt himself to be that tender husband and acted the part. Thus in the Edinburgh home of Mary Jane's family, before her relatives, he had the coffin reopened, that he might take one last look at the woman whom he had murdered; with a show of great feeling, we are told, he bent over and kissed the lips of the dead woman.

The world was Edward's stage; Edward was more than the principal actor; he was the only one; all others were there like inanimate properties, merely to enhance his importance.

It is my opinion that Edward believed he was as he saw himself to be at a particular time; it was not so much hypocrisy as that unbalanced state of mind which made him see himself as he wished to be, and to accept that aspect of himself as the true one.

In that characteristic he diverged from Cesare and Marie de Brinvilliers merely because, I think, he lived in a different world, a world closer to our own in which life was precious and not to be taken lightly even by the rich and powerful.

So he kissed the lips of his victim and wept with her family.

*   *   *

What mood was Edward in when he stepped from the train at Queen Street Station on his return to Glasgow? One of exultation surely. He would have walked out into the street like a conqueror. He had done that which he had set out to do; he had overcome all difficulties. Mrs. Taylor had dared stand in his way and he had flicked her out of it, and out of his life. Mary Jane had become an encumbrance, and alas, poor Mary Jane, she had to go also.

Now his objects were achieved. He must have thought of all those doctors who had caused him uneasiness—Cowan, Gairdner, Paterson—and considered them fools.

But perhaps he was still acting the role of bereaved husband. Perhaps he had already forgotten the sudden death of Mrs. Taylor, the agony of Mary Jane, the narcotic sleep of Elizabeth M'Girn.

Whatever his thoughts, it must have been a great shock when he stepped out of the station and felt a hand on his shoulder.

He turned and saw a man standing behind him. The man explained in a brisk voice that he was Superintendent M'Call, and that he was arresting Edward on suspicion of murdering Mary Jane Pritchard.

*　　　　*　　　　*

The fact was that while Edward was indulging in the pathetic scene by Mary Jane's coffin, an anonymous letter had arrived at the office of the Procurator-Fiscal.

It ran as follows:

Glasgow, 18th March, 1865.

Sir,—Dr. Pritchard's mother-in-law died suddenly and unexpectedly about three weeks ago in his house in Sauchiehall Street Glasgow under circumstances at least very suspicious.

His wife died today, also suddenly and unexpectedly and under circumstances equally suspicious. We think it right to direct your attention to the above as the proper person to take action in the matter and see justice done.

Amor Justitiae.

It was never discovered who sent this letter, although strong suspicion points to Dr. Paterson. He denied this, however, but there seems a strong case for believing that he may have felt it his duty both to send the letter and to deny sending it.

It enabled the authorities to search the house in Sauchiehall

Street during Edward's absence and take away various drugs which were found in the consulting room.

Later an examination took place of Mary Jane's body and it was discovered that death was not due to natural causes.

The household was questioned, and it was not long before the police discovered the relationship between Edward and Mary M'Leod; and Mary was taken into custody as being concerned in the murder of her mistress.

When the *post-mortem* examination on Mrs. Taylor's body was made it was revealed that she had died from the effects of opium which were quickened and increased by the addition of a still stronger narcotic and more stupefying poison—aconite; traces of antimony were found in her body.

There could be no doubt now that both Mrs. Taylor and her daughter, Mary Jane Pritchard, had been murdered.

*   *   *

When Edward was arrested he expressed his amazement at the charge brought against him. From the moment Superintendent M'Call took him into custody he had been so calm that all who came into contact with him felt that he must be innocent. While he was in the North Prison he spent a good deal of his time in prayer—very calm and confident—as though he were certain that a man as upright as himself could not fail to prove his innocence; he also seemed determined to impress those about him with his culture and his charm, determined to show them how foolish, how unseemly it was to bring such a diabolical charge against a man such as he was. His inordinate vanity did become obvious when he asked for a little pomatum for his hair and beard; this was denied him and he showed how angry he was, as though he were wondering how he was going to maintain that show of gracious charm without these adjuncts to his good looks.

Letters and his diary were examined. In the first days of the enquiry it had been disconcerting to read certain extracts from the diary. It must have seemed difficult to believe that this smooth-tongued man with the gentle manners could be guilty of such callous murder; but on reading the entry he had made in his diary the day Mary Jane died, it seemed almost fantastic.

18 Saturday.

Died here at 1 a.m. Mary Jane, my own beloved wife, aged 38 years—no torment surrounded her bedside—but, like a calm peaceful lamb of God—passed Minnie away. (*Minnie was a pet name occasionally used for Mary Jane by*

Edward.) May God and Jesus, Holy Gh., one in three—welcome Minnie. Prayer on prayer till mine be o'er; everlasting love. Save us, Lord, for Thy dear Son.

What sort of man was this who could submit his wife—who had done all in her power to bring nothing but good to him—to acute suffering brought about by tartar emetic and aconite, and then write such hypocritical words in his diary?

One naturally asks why he made such an entry. Was it in case there should be an enquiry and he thought this would help to prove him innocent? Or was it because he had perfected the art of seeing himself as he wished to see himself, and when he wrote those words he really believed what he wrote?

I think there was a little of both. When a person lives in a perpetual dream, the true personality might become smothered by the dream one. The true personality is, of course, the one which directs its owner's life; but deceit is second nature, and it is enacted with such a subconscious naïvety that it becomes difficult even for the possessor of this complex character to detect the duplicity at times.

In his letter to Dr. Michael Taylor who, during the last weeks of Mary Jane's illness was writing regularly to Edward asking news of his sister, Edward wrote:

No sleep came to her (*Mary Jane's*) longing wish last night—and oft she woke me—to know why no slumber came. This is very trying to her and more heartrending to me.

But this is a different matter from the diary entries. Naturally he must ward off the suspicions of Mary Jane's brother; yet the language, the pseudo-poetic language, when we know the facts, suggests a certain delight in the deceit, even delight in the suffering he is inflicting on Mary Jane.

Then again we ask ourselves what was the motive for this diabolical murder? Could this man have watched the terrible suffering of his wife, knowing he had brought about that suffering, with equanimity, with a hypocritical pretence of sympathy which he describes as 'heartrending', if he had not passionately desired her death?

Yet why should he so passionately have desired the death of Mary Jane? She was docile. She caused him little trouble. Did he really want to marry Mary M'Leod? It seems incredible that he should. A man of his extreme vanity to marry a servant girl when class differences were far more sharply defined than they are today! Where was the urgency? Mary M'Leod was already his most willing mistress.

It is said that the real motive for Edward Pritchard's destroying his wife has never been discovered.

His financial position was bad, but he stood to gain very little by the death of his wife and mother-in-law. Cesare Borgia ordered people to be murdered who might be considered beneath his notice. "Let this one die because he witnessed certain humiliation which I suffered and may talk of it." That was enough. It was easier in those days. Cesare had his band of assassins and did not have to answer for his crimes. Marie de Brinvilliers showed the same indifference to life as Cesare did. When she wanted to test the efficacy of a poison she tried it out on a victim selected from the most convenient place. It was not important to her that a life was ended through her actions; all that mattered was whether the person died quickly, slowly, or not at all.

I believe that Edward Pritchard, Cesare Borgia and Madame de Brinvilliers were similar in this respect.

Edward destroyed those three women because each of them threatened to destroy something which he treasured: his image of himself, the picture of what he wished himself to be.

Elizabeth M'Girn, when she must have hinted at some form of blackmail, metaphorically held up a picture for him to see— Edward Pritchard, seducer of a humble servant girl, liar and deceiver. It was quite a different picture from that one of himself which Edward treasured, the charming personality of the club and lecture hall, Mary Jane's affectionate husband, a man devoted to his children—in fact an admirable person. Elizabeth M'Girn laid another picture over that one, and, because he recognized, if only for a short time, the truth of hers and the falseness of his own, she had to die.

Mary Jane did a similar thing. She discovered Mary M'Leod and her husband kissing in a bedroom; she knew Mary M'Leod had had an abortion which had been procured by Edward. Mary Jane had destroyed the picture of affectionate husband and devoted family man. Edward could not live with a woman who had glimpsed him as he really was. He wanted someone who could not only give him sexual satisfaction, as could the young and lusty, yet simple, Mary M'Leod; he wanted some-one who would always see him as he wanted to be seen. That was why, after Mary Jane had discovered him with the servant, he talked to Mary M'Leod of marriage.

As for Mrs. Taylor, her destruction of his beautiful picture was quicker and more revealing than any of the others. Her maternal instincts had sharpened her wits; she had not been in the house very long when she must have suspected her daughter was being poisoned, and when she came upon Edward and Mary M'Leod in an equivocal situation, she may have linked the suffering of Mary Jane with this. Mrs. Taylor was doomed from that moment. Edward realized that he would be committing the supreme folly if he let her live. Here was a really practical motive, which immediately occurs to the casual enquirer. But she, too, had destroyed the picture which Edward showed the Taylors, and she died for that, as well as for the reason that she was on the point of discovering who was poisoning Mary Jane.

* * *

During the weeks which followed, Edward showed a brave face to the world and insisted on declaring his innocence.

The trial opened on 3rd July, and there was great public interest. This was partly due to the fact that Dr. Paterson told the jury that when he had visited Mrs. Pritchard he had suspected she was being poisoned. He was severely reprimanded for doing nothing about this, and reminded that, had he done something, he might have saved Mrs. Pritchard's life. His insistence on the etiquette of the medical profession brought him nothing but ridicule, and this case had a decidedly adverse effect upon his career.

Further interest was aroused when Andrew Rutherfurd Clark, who was defending Edward, tried to pin the murders on to Mary M'Leod. Poor little Mary was a pitiable figure in the witness box, being forced to admit her intimacy with the doctor, the discovery in the bedroom, and the doctor's suggestion that he might marry her if his wife died.

It may have been that during those days Edward believed that Providence had once again come to his aid and was offering little Mary M'Leod as a sacrifice to justice.

But there was the Solicitor-General to thunder out his questions: "Do you think a girl of seventeen could have done this deed? Did she know anything about antimony? If she did not, the prisoner must have done it."

The conclusion was inevitable. Mary M'Leod was released, and the jury found Edward William Pritchard guilty of both charges as libelled.

He was sentenced to be taken to a common place of execution and there by the hands of the executioner, be hanged by the neck upon a gibbet until he was dead.

* * *

Edward was true to his character during the days when he was awaiting his end. He was angry with Mary M'Leod, for as he began to see it, since he himself was above guilt, Mary was the guilty one. Had Mary M'Leod not come to the house, Mary Jane would be alive. That was how he had always reasoned. There was a new picture to build of himself. His kindness to Mary M'Leod had been abused. He had thought of her as poor Mary from a humble home, who needed him; he had thought that she would make a good mother for his children, as poor, ailing Mary Jane could not be. He would convince himself that Mary M'Leod was the true killer.

He wrote a 'confession' in which he accused Mary of complicity. He had been living, he wrote, in a 'species of madness since his connection with Mary M'Leod'. He wrote that Mary M'Leod knew that Mrs. Pritchard was being poisoned, and that she had been present when the last and fatal dose had been given.

This confession was held to be false and it was not made public; but later, the priest who visited him in prison urged him not to die in falsehood; and Edward's picture changed suddenly. He saw himself as the man who had been guilty of great crime and folly, yet was determined to go nobly to his death. He repudiated the first confession and wrote another, and in this he said that he alone, not Mary M'Leod, was guilty.

* * *

On 28th July, 1865, Edward Pritchard was publicly hanged on the Green in front of the South Jail. Crowds came in, as was the custom, from Bridgegate and the Saltmarket and from all the little streets of Glasgow to witness the show. Vendors of pies, drinks, gingerbread, ballads and broadsheets, assembled there; and all through the night, the crowds waited. They saw the scaffold erected and the coffin brought out and placed beside it.

And in the morning Edward emerged from the prison. Edward was safe in his dignity, for even at this moment it would not have been the real Edward whom he showed to the waiting crowds, not Edward the poisoner, but Edward the calm, handsome, cultured man who had sinned and was going to show them how a gentleman went to his death.

He stood still while the cap was drawn over his face, his legs tied and the rope placed round his neck. In that moment there would be no longer the need to pose before the world, for the white cap hid his face. What did he feel in those seconds? Would he think fleetingly of the death sleep of Elizabeth M'Girn, of the suffering of Jane Taylor and of the even more acute agony of Mary Jane?

There would have been little time for reflection.

THE VERDICT

An ANALYSIS of the characters of these three poisoners offers one certain conclusion. They lived in completely different times; their environment and upbringing were quite dissimilar; and yet, in all three characters there is that recognizable trait of murderous inclination.

It seems to have its roots in one characteristic: Egoism. This is, of course, a natural human characteristic, possessed in some degree by us all; but these murderers were all remarkable for their unrestrained egoism, a monstrous egoism, which grew like a cancer in the body until it first dominated and then destroyed. It is a fantastic egoism; it would be quite ridiculous if not so tragic for all those—including its possessors—who came within its range.

To all of my three poisoners no person was of any significance, except in relation to themselves. Cesare had no compunction in murdering Alfonso of Bisceglie, although he was fully aware of Lucrezia's affection for her husband; yet Cesare was passionately attached to Lucrezia. Cesare's devotion to his sister existed solely in her importance to him. Therefore, six weeks after he had murdered her husband, he visited her and expected to be— and in fact was—received as her beloved brother.

Marie de Brinvilliers was passionately in love with Gaudin de Sainte-Croix, but he knew that he must at times be on the alert lest she try to poison him.

Edward Pritchard was in love with Mary M'Leod, but he, like Cesare Borgia and Marie de Brinvilliers, was incapable of selfless love because he too could not imagine an existence in which he was not of sole importance. He protected Mary while she was in his house, but that was because he had found that Mary could give him more pleasure than anyone else. When he was in prison and saw a means of escape from justice he allowed his counsel to bring a charge against Mary which might have shifted the blame from his shoulders to hers. So much for his love. But it is easy to understand why he could do this. Mary was no longer of any use to him; she was, therefore, of no importance whatsoever. Let her take the blame. It was a way out; and the world was made for Edward Pritchard. Edward was quite ready to throw the girl whom he had professed to love over to the hangman, if by so doing he could save himself. Cesare would have thrown Lucrezia in the same way; Marie would have thrown Sainte-Croix.

They could not love others. How could they? It was part of the natures which made them what they were, that all the love of which they were capable was for themselves.

If Edward Pritchard had been born into Cesare Borgia's position he would have killed, I believe, in the same careless way; so would Marie de Brinvilliers. And if Cesare and Marie had been Glasgow doctors faced with Edward's problems, they would have decided that first Elizabeth M'Girn, then Mrs. Taylor, and then Mary Jane must die.

These murderers did not look at life as does the ordinary sane person. Therefore it is not always easy to find a straight-forward motive for their crimes.

Cesare would murder because he did not like a man's facial expression when he spoke his name; Marie was equally nonchalant in the use of her poison. The murders of father and brothers, the attempted murders of sister and sister-in-law, have strong motives; but Marie would poison for a light whim. When she was irritated by the dullness and plainness of one of her daughters she gave the poor child a dose of poison; one day it lightly occurred to her that she would like to marry Sainte-Croix, so there was a dose for the Marquis. Edward was more cautious with his lethal doses; but that seems to be solely due to the fact that he was living in a later age when there was more chance of exposure and retribution.

It is only fair to point out that these people all met their deaths bravely, which is what one would expect of them. They were not cowards; all of them readily took great risks.

Cesare, fighting at Viana, when leading his men into battle outstripped them and so fell to the enemy. He died as a brave soldier would die; and there are some who declare that his death was a form of suicide, as it was no accident that he had ridden on ahead of his men. Cesare who had dealt death to many was not afraid of it himself.

Marie was brave and uncomplaining under torture; she was stoically patient while the executioner slowly cut her hair and prepared her for the knife. She faced the assembly in the Place de Grève with calm courage.

And thus it was with Edward. He too was brave and showed no fear when he was brought out of the prison and publicly hanged on the Green in front of the Glasgow South Jail.

Edward had then, as he had through life, seen the man he wished himself to be rather than the man he was: Handsome, brave to the end. He had confessed, but it was typical of him that he should ask that his confession should not be made public until after the execution, feeling that many of those in the crowd gathered there to see him die, would believe him innocent and very noble. Thus the picture would survive until the end.

What makes a man or woman commit murder? Is it environment? Marie's sister, the Carmelite nun, would have been brought up in the same way as Marie was; yet how different were these sisters! Marie had planned to poison the Carmelite in order that she might take her share of the family fortune. When the Carmelite, knowing what Marie's plans had been, heard that her criminal sister was hiding in Liège, she sent money to her that she might live in quiet comfort. Why should two sisters be so different if environment makes the murderer?

Edward Pritchard was a callous murderer, yet members of his family, who had been brought up with him, were kind and gentle people.

In Cesare's case it is less easy to defend the suggestion: Environment does not make the murderer. He was born into a particularly barbarous age, and was surrounded by unscrupulous men and women; but surely Cesare stands out among them as especially brutal and callous. Lucrezia seems gentle in comparison; and even Pope Alexander showed affection and tenderness for some. We hear of the terrible Borgia poison when Cesare comes of age; and Alexander, although emerging as a man governed by sensuality and ambition, considering his times had certain good qualities.

And Cesare had so much in common with Edward and Marie. Time and conditions may divide them, but I feel that if they had lived in any time, in any circumstances, they would have come to murder. They are as one and the same person even though there are certain individual characteristics attached to each: Cesare's barbarity; Marie's reckless extravagance; Edward's hypocrisy. Cesare lived in a barbarous age; Marie lived in an extravagant one; and surely Edward's times were the most hypocritical through which Britain has ever passed.

The three murderers wear these characteristics as they would wear the satin doublets, slashed with gold, the flattering 'mouches' on the face, the luxuriant beard. These were the fashions of the day, and would have been discarded when the fashion changed. But the real men, the real woman, would never change.

This is my verdict: The guilt belongs, not to their contemporaries, but to the murderers.

They alone have the power to adjust their visions; they alone can prick the dangerous bubble of their self-esteem; they alone can destroy it before it destroys their victims and themselves.

WORKS CONSULTED

The Outline of Italian Civilization. Decio Pettoello.

History of the Italian Republics in the Middle Ages. J. C. L. Sismondi. Recast and Supplemented in the light of Historical Research by William Boulting.

Cesare Borgia. Charles Yriarte. Translated by William Stirling.

Cesare Borgia. William Harrison Woodward.

Lucrezia Borgia: A Chapter from the Morals of the Italian Renaissance. Ferdinand Gregorovius.

Lucrezia Borgia. Joan Haslip.

The Life and Times of Lucrezia Borgia. Maria Bellonci. Translated by Bernard Wall.

The Marriage at Ferrara. Simon Harcourt-Smith.

France. William Henry Hudson.

The Old Régime in France. Frantz Funck-Brentano.

The History of France. M. Guizot. Translated by Robert Black.

Madame de Brinvilliers and her Times, 1630-1676. Hugh Stokes.

The Marchioness of Brinvilliers. Albert Smith.

Trial of Dr. Pritchard. (Notable Scottish Trials Series.) Edited by William Roughead.

The Book of Poisons. Gustav Schenk. Translated by Michael Bullock.

INDEX

INDEX

Racine, Jean, 80
René, the Florentine, 76, 77, 90
Riario, Girolamo, 18
Richelieu, Armand Jean Duplessis, Cardinal de, 76
Rovere, Giuliano della, Pope Julius II, 27, 36, 37, 71, 72
Ruggieri Brothers, 76, 77

Sainte-Croix, Gaudin de, 82-119, 121, 124, 127, 129, 184, 185
Sainte-Croix, Madame de, 91, 117, 119
Saint-Laurent, 115, 116
Saint-Laurent, Madame de, 116, 119, 122
Sanchia of Aragon, 33, 34, 41-3, 45, 49, 53, 54, 58, 63-6
Savonarola, Girolamo, 38
Scudéry, Georges de, 80
Scudéry, Madeleine de, 80
Sévigné, Marquise de, 127, 129
Sforza, Ascanio Maria, Cardinal, 27, 29, 37
Sforza, Caterina, Countess of Forli, 60, 61

Sforza, Duke Galeazzo Maria, 60
Sforza, Giovanni, Count of Cotignola, Lord of Pesaro, 29-32, 37-8, 40, 43, 45, 46, 49, 50, 53
Sforza, Ludovico, Duke of Milan, 27, 29, 46, 57, 62
Sixtus IV, Pope, 18, 19, 27
Smith, Madeleine, 153, 154

Taylor, Jane, 135-8, 142, 147, 148, 153, 155-7, 162, 163, 166-74, 176-9, 181-3, 185
Taylor, Michael, 132, 135, 137, 138, 142, 148, 172
Taylor, Dr. Michael, 136-8, 142, 148, 163, 164, 165, 166, 174, 180

Vallot, physician to Anne of Austria, 92
Verona Gaspare da, 15
Victor Emmanuel, 139
Voisin, La, 129
Volterra, Jacopo da, 23

0352 Star

301392	Linda Blandford **OIL SHEIKHS**	95p
396121	Anthony Cave Brown **BODYGUARD OF LIES (Large Format)**	£1.95*
301368	John Dean **BLIND AMBITION**	£1.00*
300124	Dr. F. Dodson **HOW TO PARENT**	75p*
301457	**THE FAMILY DICTIONARY OF SYMPTOMS**	95p*
398914	J. Paul Getty **HOW TO BE RICH**	60p*
397829	**HOW TO BE A SUCCESSFUL EXECUTIVE**	60p*
398566	Harry Lorayne & Jerry Lucas **THE MEMORY BOOK**	60p*
39692X	Henry Miller **THE WORLD OF SEX**	60p
395311	Neville Randall & Gary Keane **FOCUS ON FACT:** **THE WORLD OF INVENTION (illus)**	75p
39532X	**THE STORY OF SPORT (illus)**	75p
39529X	**THE PSYCHIC WORLD (illus)**	75p
395303	**THE STORY OF CHRISTMAS (illus)**	75p
395338	**UNSOLVED MYSTERIES (illus)**	75p
397640	David Reuben **HOW TO GET MORE OUT OF SEX**	85p*
398779	Fiona Richmond **FIONA**	50p
396040	Idries Shah **THE SUFIS (Large Format)**	£1.95
395478	Michael Smith **THE DUCHESS OF DUKE STREET** **ENTERTAINS**	£1.50♦

† For sale in Britain and Ireland only.
* Not for sale in Canada.
♦ Film & T.V. tie-ins.

GENERAL NON-FICTION

0426	Universal/Tandem	
	Thomas B. Costain **THE PAGEANT OF ENGLAND:**	
123190	**1135-1216: THE CONQUERING FAMILY**	£1.50
123271	**1216-1272: THE MAGNIFICENT CENTURY**	£1.50
123352	**1272-1377: THE THREE EDWARDS**	£1.50
123433	**1377-1485: THE LAST PLANTAGENETS**	£1.50
184033	Ben Davidson **THE OFFICIAL FONZIE SCRAPBOOK**	70p* ♦
08571X	Hyam Maccoby **REVOLUTION IN JUDAEA**	75p
168623	Xaviera Hollander **THE HAPPY HOOKER**	80p*
163443	**LETTERS TO THE HAPPY HOOKER**	80p*
168038	**XAVIERA GOES WILD**	80p*
166787	**XAVIERA ON THE BEST PART OF A MAN**	80p*
134265	**XAVIERA!**	80p*
17996X	Xaviera Hollander & Marilyn Chambers **XAVIERA MEETS MARILYN CHAMBERS**	80p*
124901	Fridtjof Nansen **FARTHEST NORTH**	£1.00
175158	Sakuzawa Nyoiti **MACROBIOTICS**	50p*
181638	Suze Randall **SUZE**	75p*
180755	Grant Tracy Saxon **THE HAPPY HUSTLER**	70p
134931	La Leche League **THE WOMANLY ART OF BREASTFEEDING**	60p
141970	Erna Wright **THE NEW CHILDBIRTH**	75p
067282	**THE NEW CHILDHOOD**	75p
054938	**PERIODS WITHOUT PAIN**	60p
0426	Hanau Distribution	
087232	David Lewis **SEXPIONAGE**	70p
087151	**THE SECRET LIFE OF ADOLPH HITLER**	75p
086864	Linda Lovelace **INSIDE LINDA LOVELACE**	60p
086945	**THE INTIMATE DIARY OF LINDA LOVELACE**	60p
086007	Gerard I. Nierenberg & Henry H. Calero **HOW TO READ A PERSON LIKE A BOOK**	95p

† For sale in Britain and Ireland only
* Not for sale in Canada
♦ Film & T.V. tie-ins

Wyndham Books are obtainable from many booksellers and newsagents. If you have any difficulty please send purchase price plus postage on the scale below to:

Wyndham Cash Sales,
P.O. Box 11,
Falmouth,
Cornwall

OR

Star Book Service,
G.P.O. Box 29,
Douglas,
Isle of Man,
British Isles

While every effort is made to keep prices low, it is sometimes necessary to increase prices at short notice. Wyndham Books reserve the right to show new retail prices on covers which may differ from those advertised in the text or elsewhere.

Postage and Packing Rate
U.K.
One book 22p plus 10p per copy for each additional book ordered to a maximum charge of 82p.

B.F.P.O. and Eire
One book 22p plus 10p per copy for the next 6 books and thereafter 4p per book. Overseas 30p for the first book and 10p per copy for each additional book.